THIS BOOK BELONGS TO

....

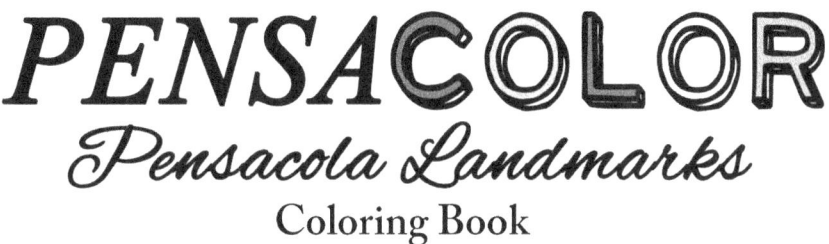

PENSACOLOR
Pensacola Landmarks
Coloring Book

Copyright 2016 by Teresa Scott Dobson

ISBN-13: 978-1523411580
ISBN-10: 1523411589

Cover and Interior Art by Teresa Scott Dobson

Editor: Matthew Dobson

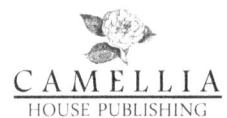

CAMELLIA
HOUSE PUBLISHING

Camellia House Publishing, Century, FL
Printed in the United States of America.

camelliahousepublishing@aol.com

BEFORE YOU GET STARTED!

1. Put away all of the worldly distractions around you -- TV, phone, computer, etc.

2. Take out some color pencils, markers or crayons.

3. Pick a page and go with it. There's no particular order to follow.

4. When you finish a design, personalize it by signing your name anywhere on the page.

5. Find the Graffiti Bridge page and create your own graffiti!

6. Find the McGuire's Irish Pub page and draw your own Leprechaun on the sign.

7. Stop when you need a break, then pick it up again later.

8. When finished, if you desire, share your creations with others!

9. One more important tip… make sure to place a blank sheet of paper in between the page designs as you color to cut down on ink bleed.

ENJOY!

We would love to see any of your finished creations! Send a picture of your art to *pensacolor@aol.com or visit us on Facebook and upload your art at PensaColor!* *(Attach jpeg files 10 megs or less per email)*

"Welcome to Pensacola, the Western gate to the Sunshine State, where thousands live the way millions wish they could, where the warmth of our community comes not only from God's good sunshine, but from the hearts of the people who live here. Welcome to Pensacola, America's first place city and the place where America began."

Vince Whibbs Sr.,
long-time Mayor of the City of Pensacola, Florida.
~1920-2006~

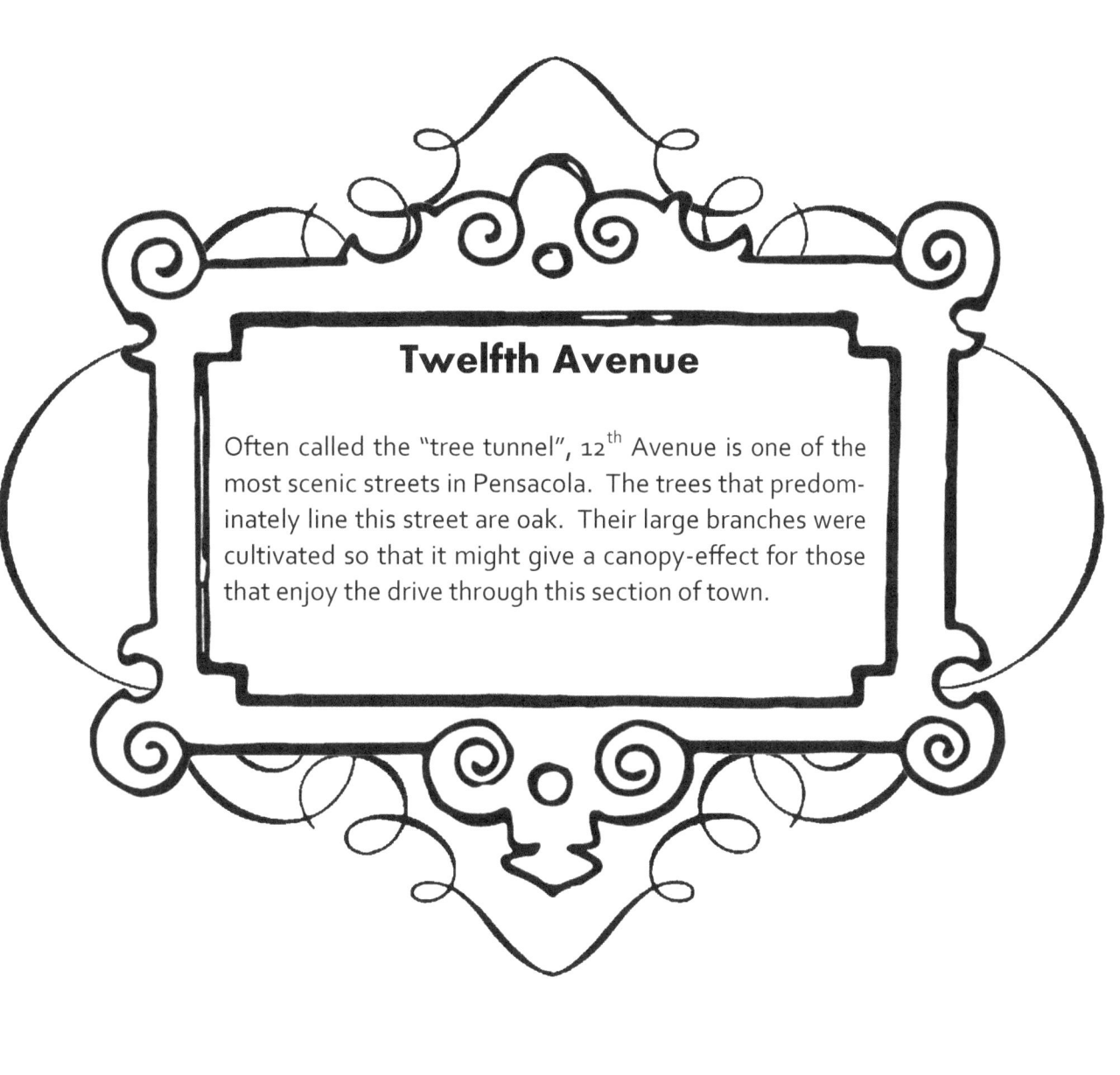

Twelfth Avenue

Often called the "tree tunnel", 12th Avenue is one of the most scenic streets in Pensacola. The trees that predominately line this street are oak. Their large branches were cultivated so that it might give a canopy-effect for those that enjoy the drive through this section of town.

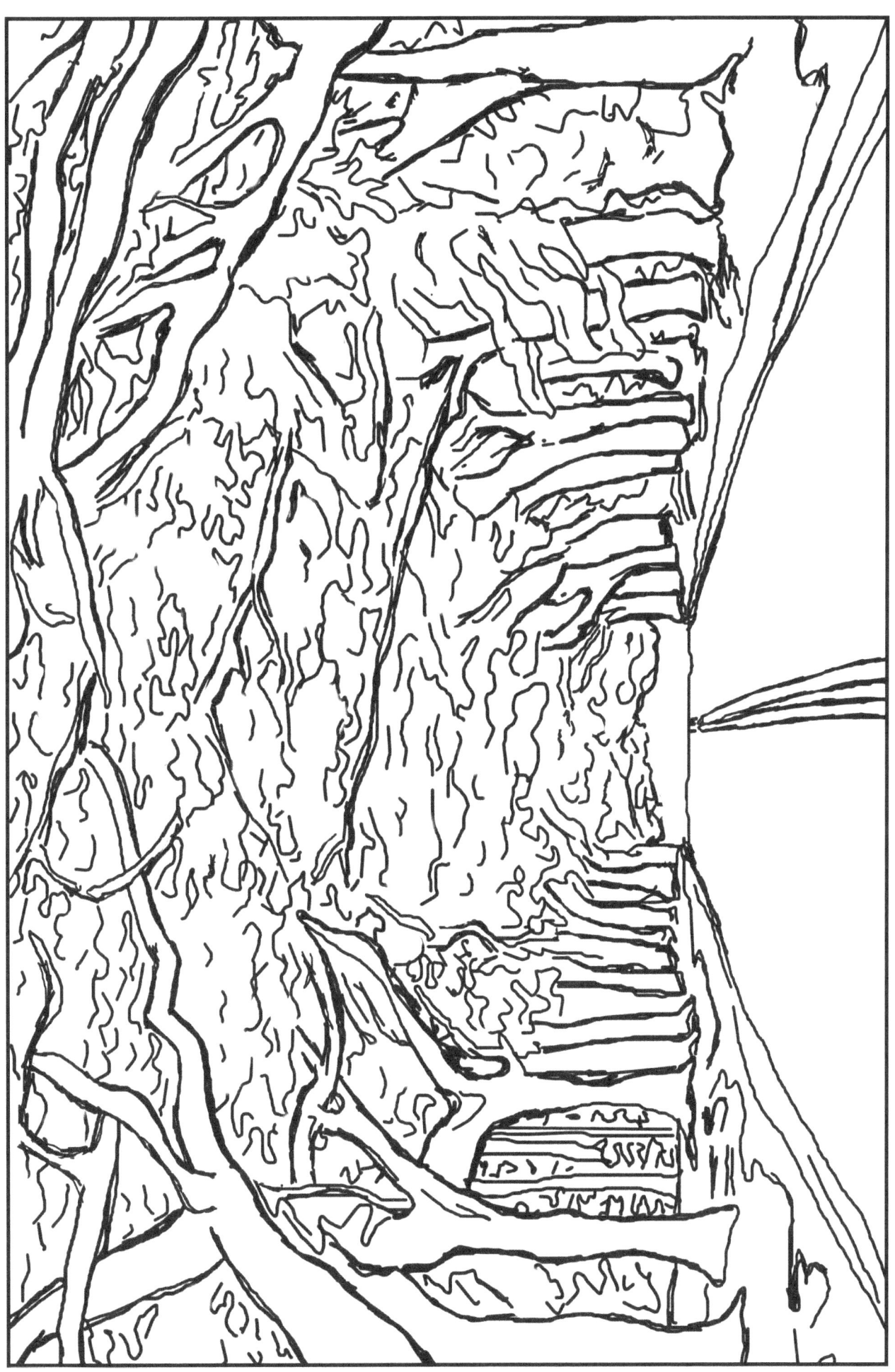

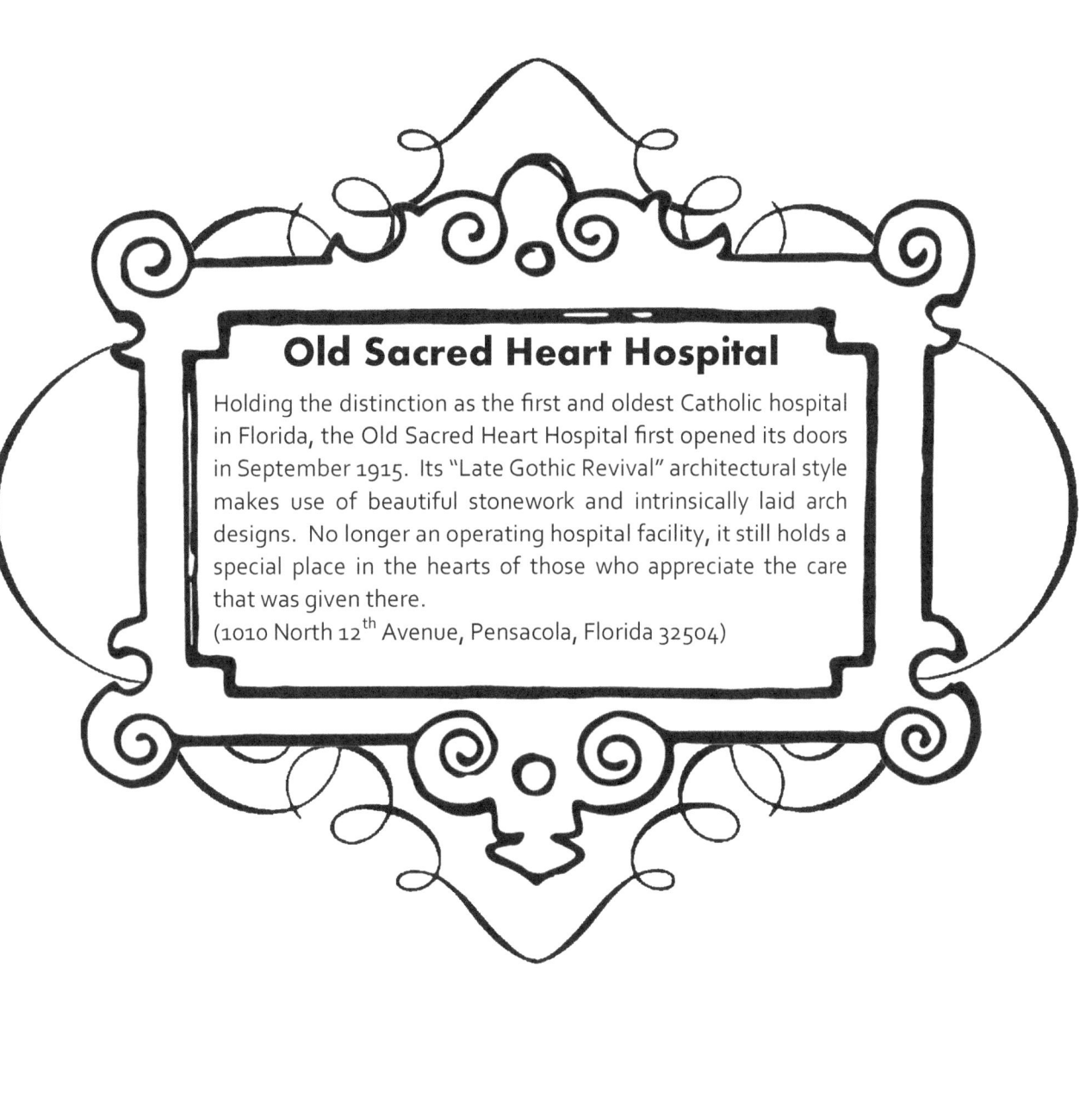

Old Sacred Heart Hospital

Holding the distinction as the first and oldest Catholic hospital in Florida, the Old Sacred Heart Hospital first opened its doors in September 1915. Its "Late Gothic Revival" architectural style makes use of beautiful stonework and intrinsically laid arch designs. No longer an operating hospital facility, it still holds a special place in the hearts of those who appreciate the care that was given there.

(1010 North 12th Avenue, Pensacola, Florida 32504)

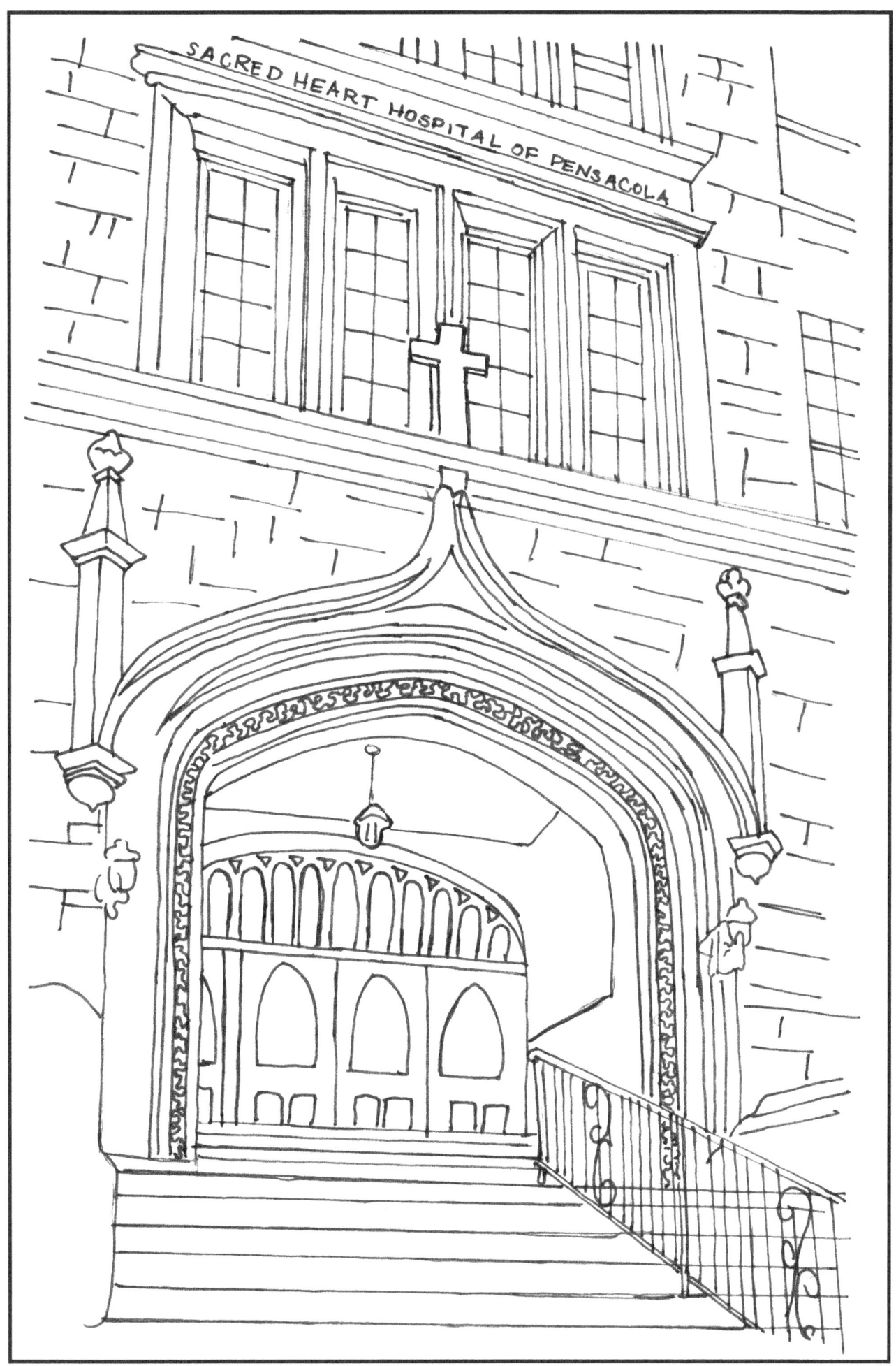

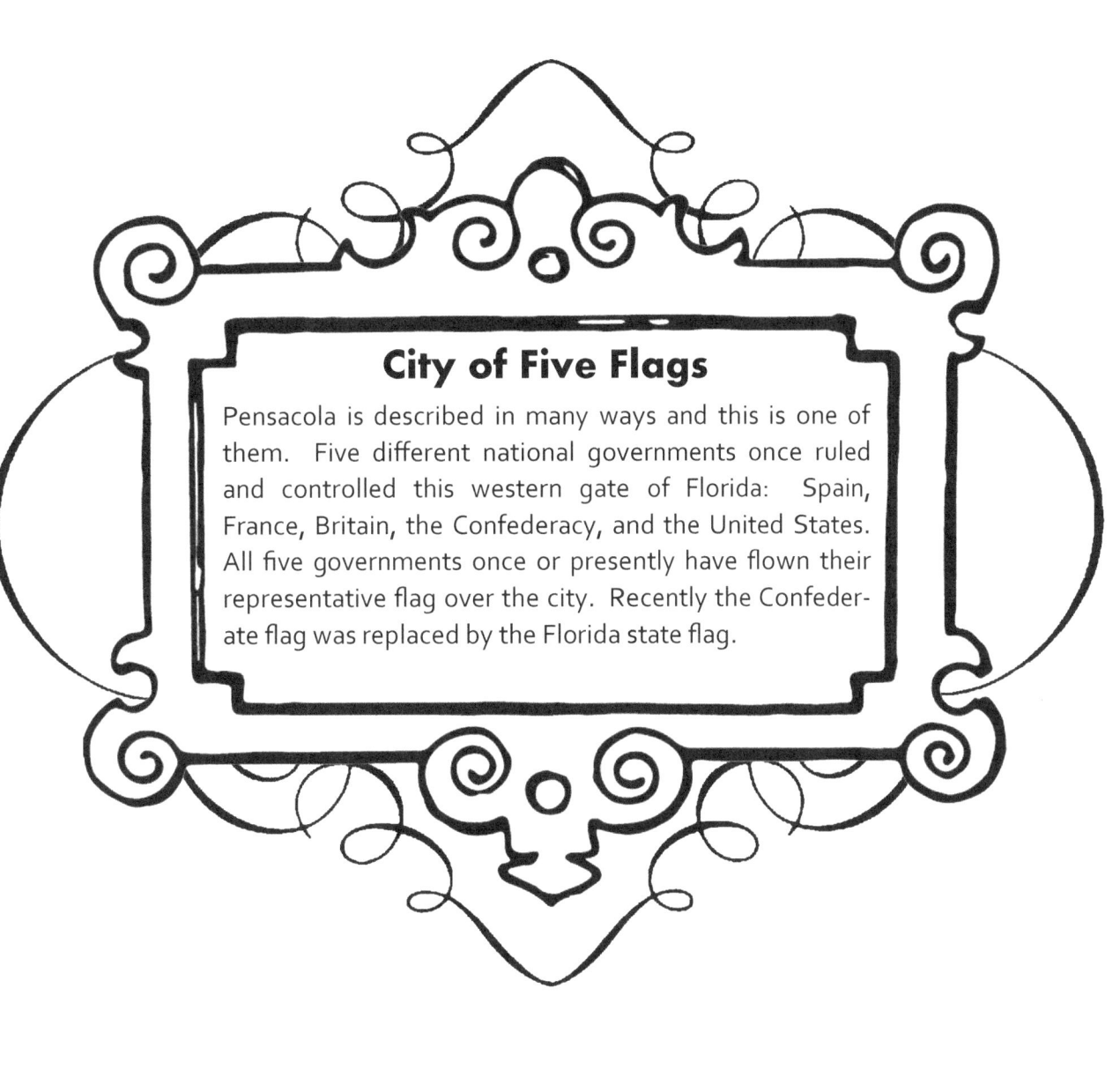

City of Five Flags

Pensacola is described in many ways and this is one of them. Five different national governments once ruled and controlled this western gate of Florida: Spain, France, Britain, the Confederacy, and the United States. All five governments once or presently have flown their representative flag over the city. Recently the Confederate flag was replaced by the Florida state flag.

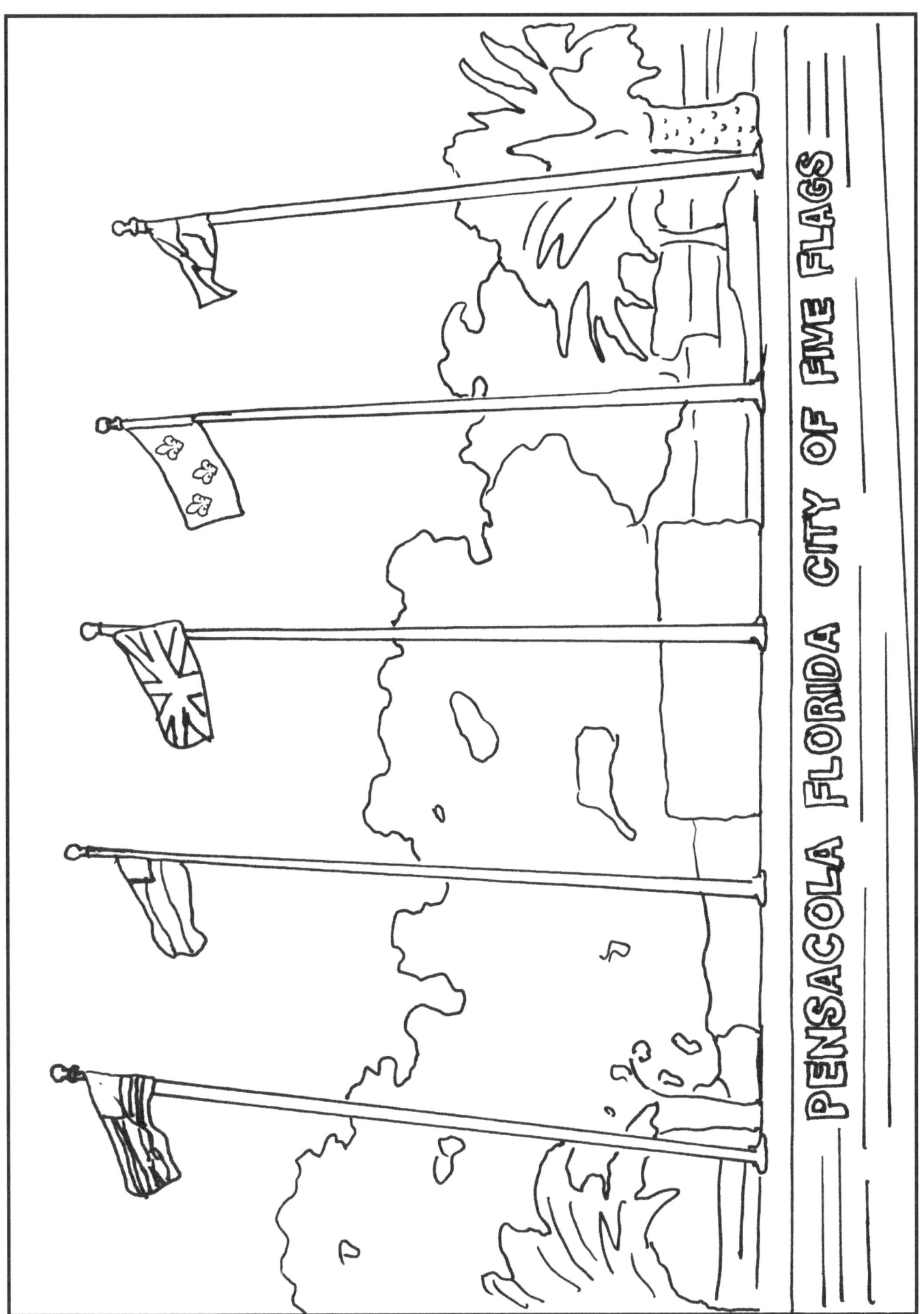

PENSACOLA FLORIDA CITY OF FIVE FLAGS

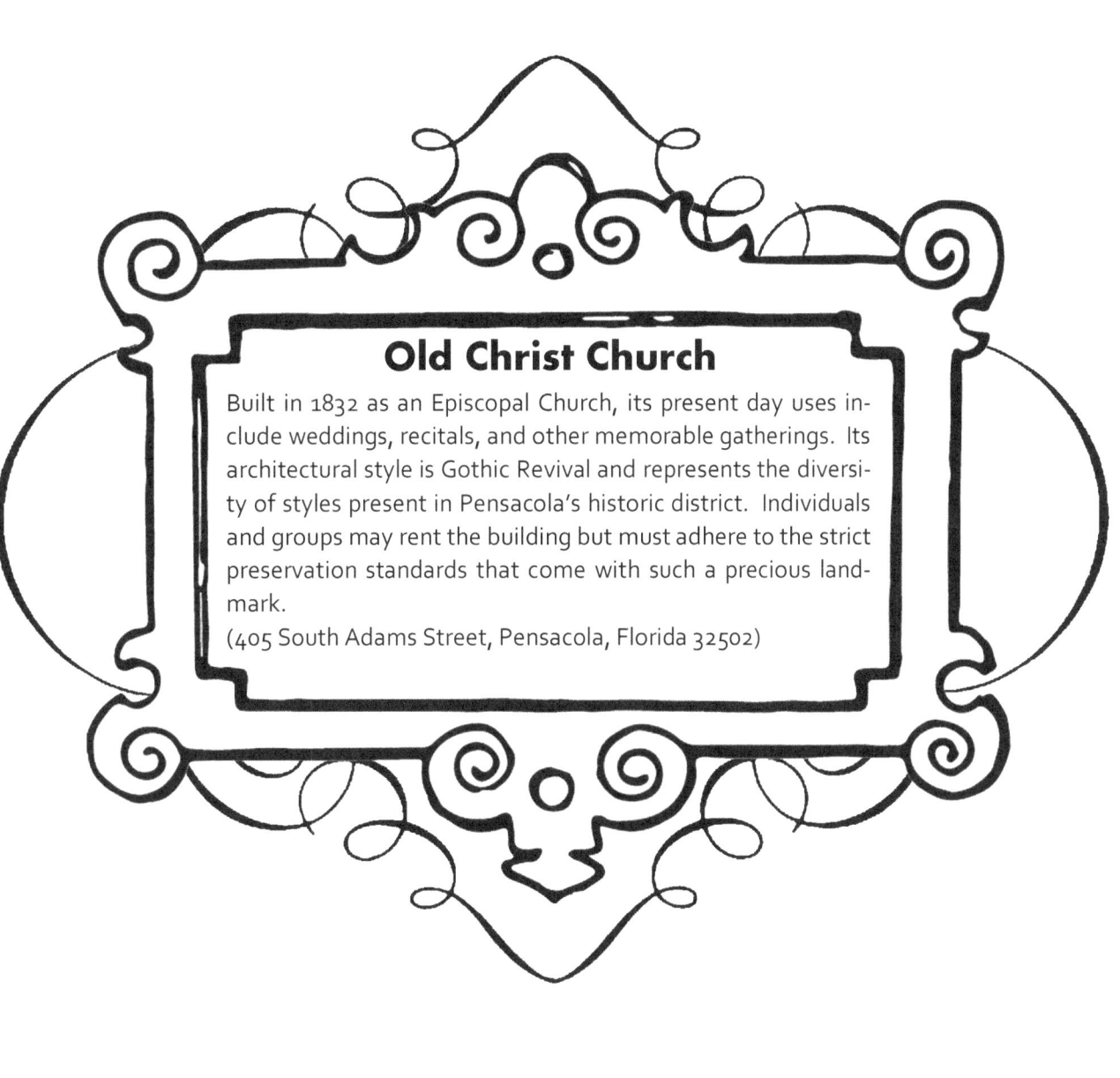

Old Christ Church

Built in 1832 as an Episcopal Church, its present day uses include weddings, recitals, and other memorable gatherings. Its architectural style is Gothic Revival and represents the diversity of styles present in Pensacola's historic district. Individuals and groups may rent the building but must adhere to the strict preservation standards that come with such a precious landmark.

(405 South Adams Street, Pensacola, Florida 32502)

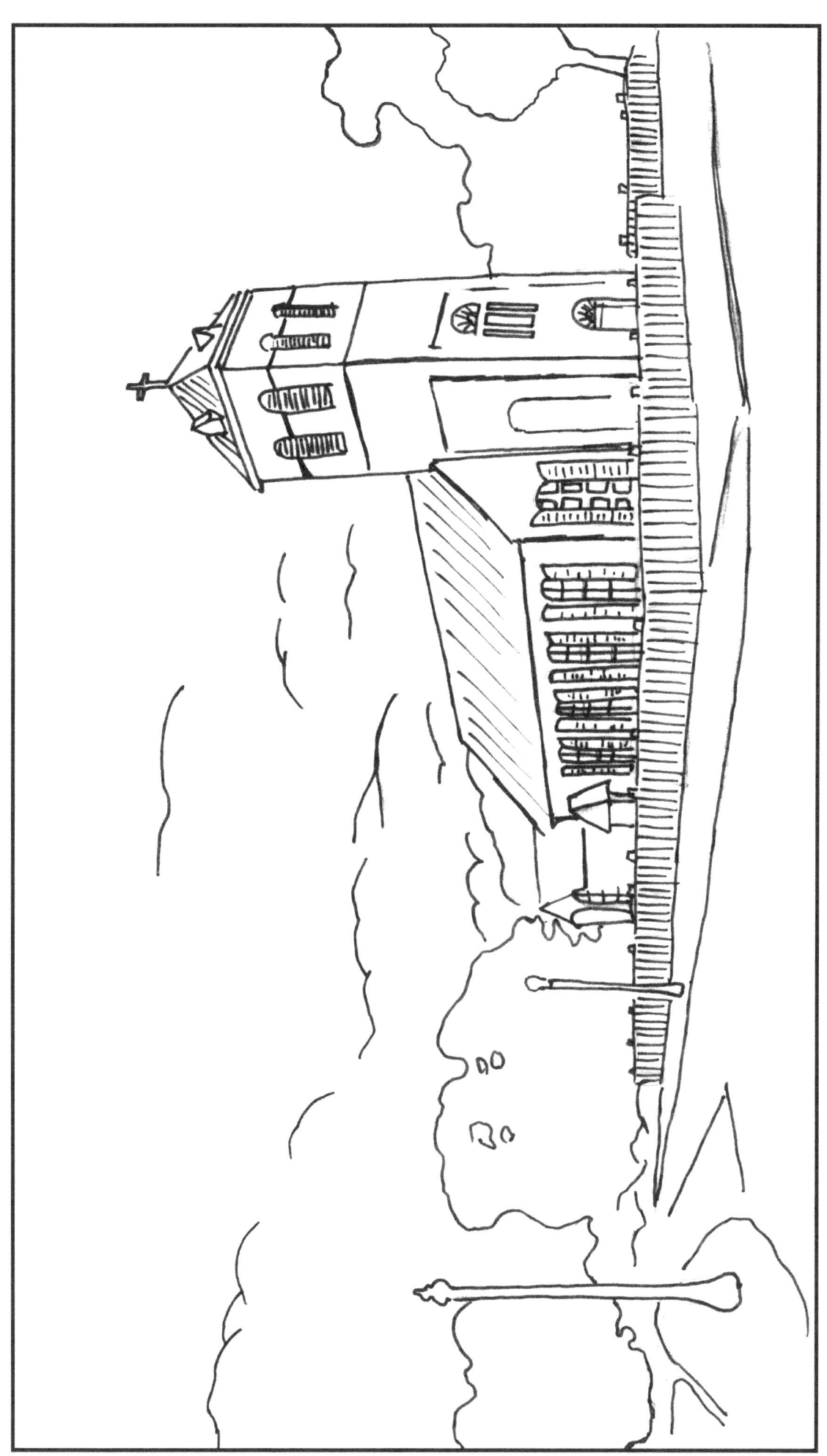

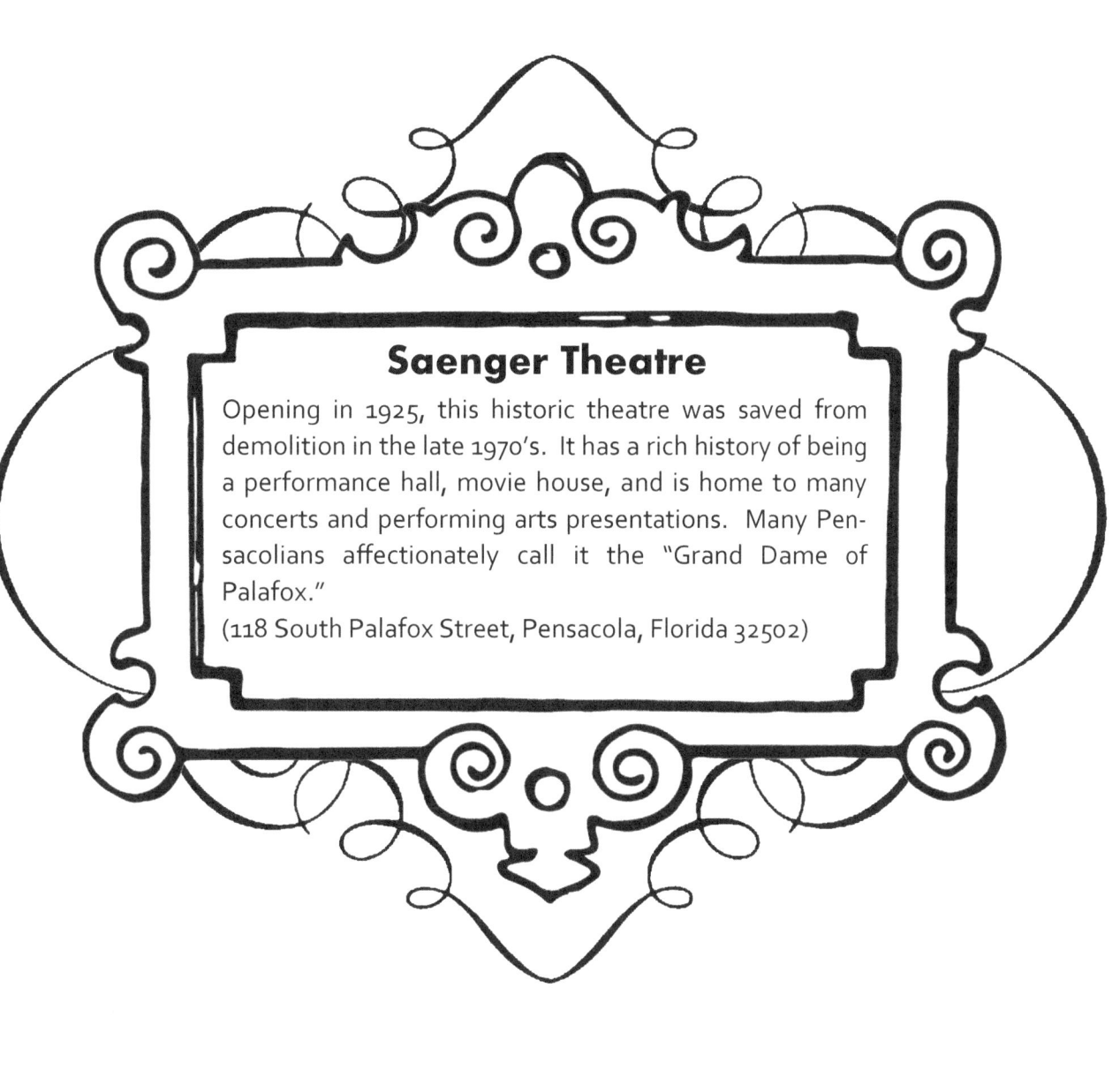

Saenger Theatre

Opening in 1925, this historic theatre was saved from demolition in the late 1970's. It has a rich history of being a performance hall, movie house, and is home to many concerts and performing arts presentations. Many Pensacolians affectionately call it the "Grand Dame of Palafox."

(118 South Palafox Street, Pensacola, Florida 32502)

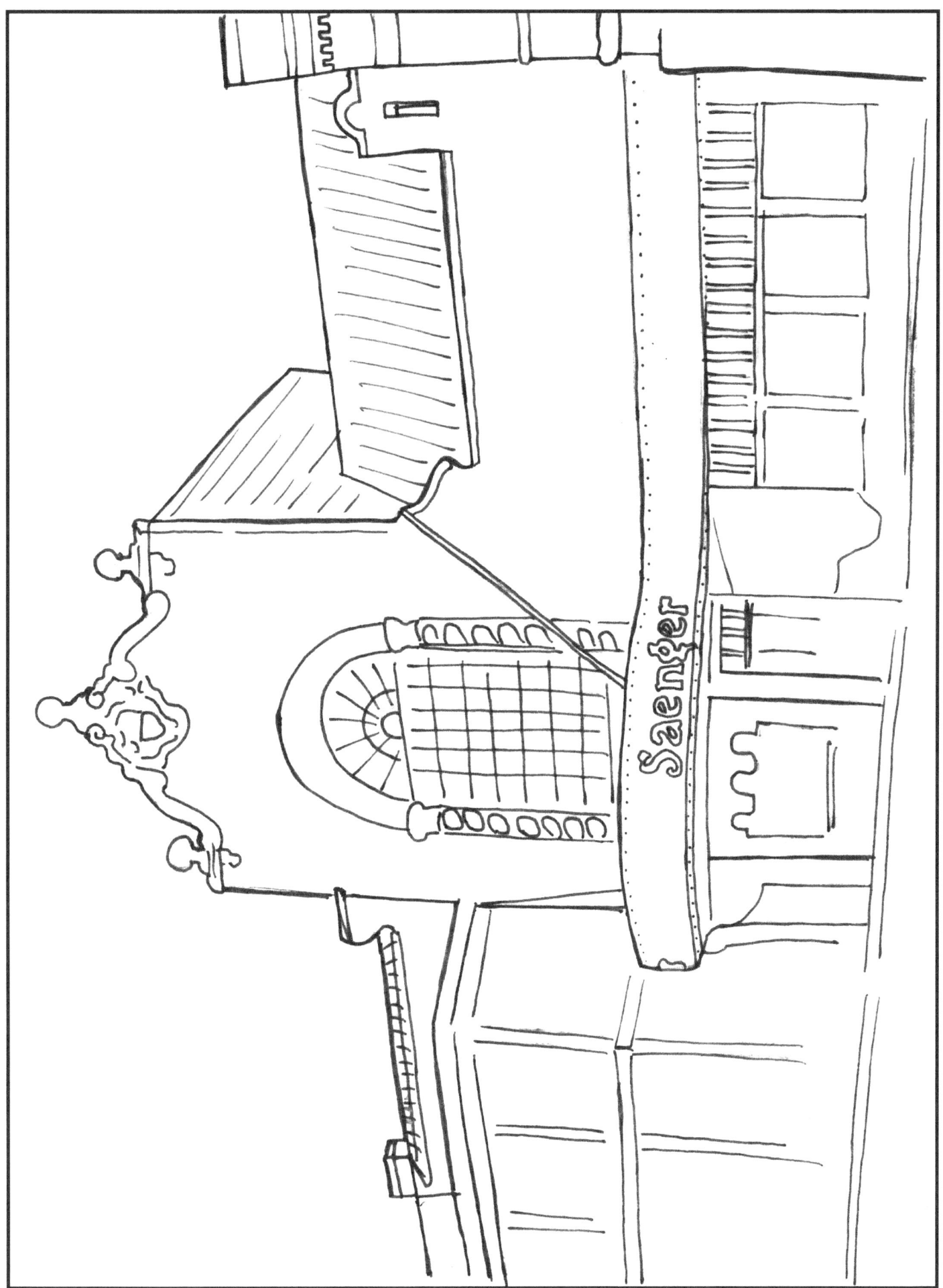

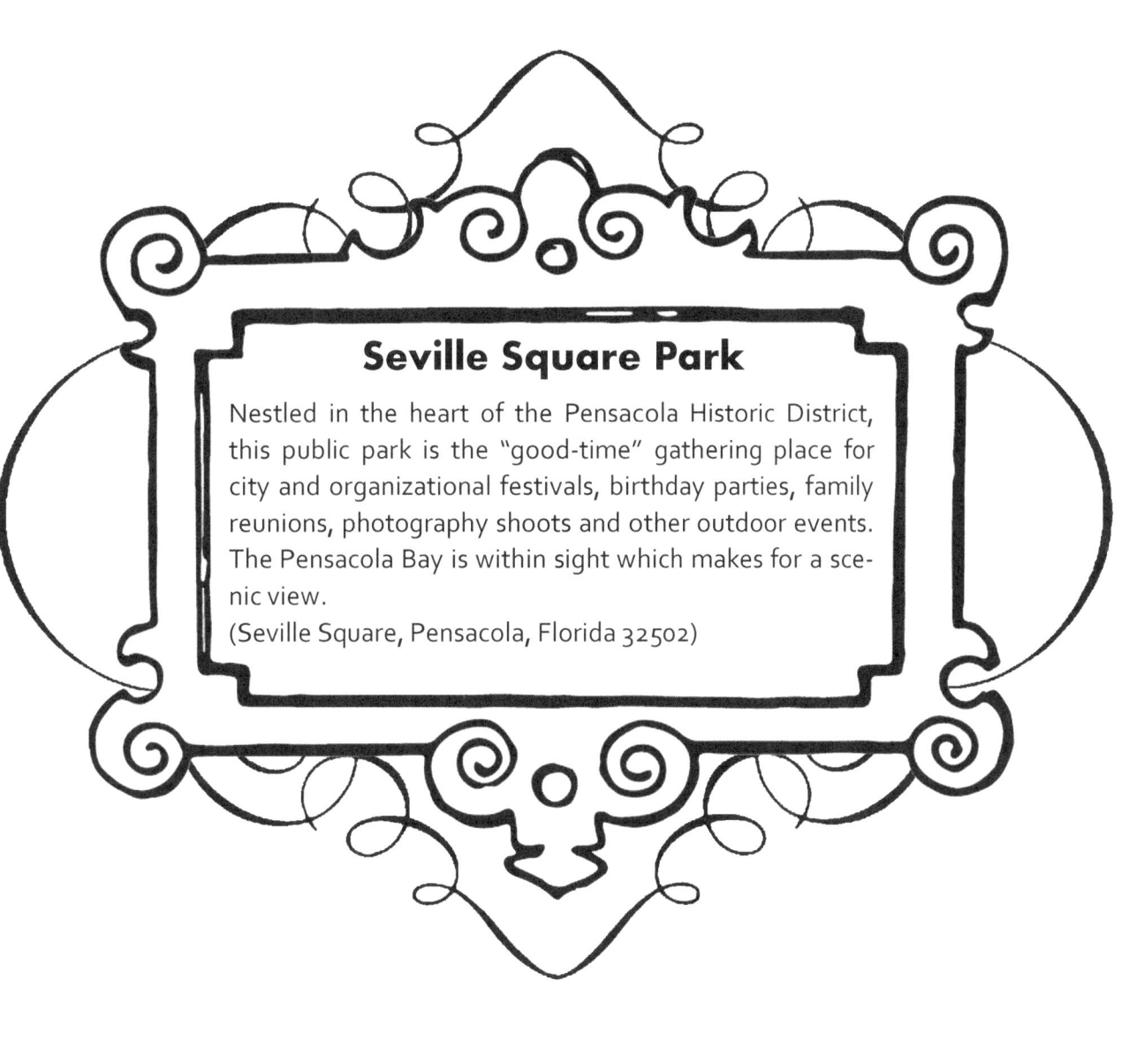

Seville Square Park

Nestled in the heart of the Pensacola Historic District, this public park is the "good-time" gathering place for city and organizational festivals, birthday parties, family reunions, photography shoots and other outdoor events. The Pensacola Bay is within sight which makes for a scenic view.

(Seville Square, Pensacola, Florida 32502)

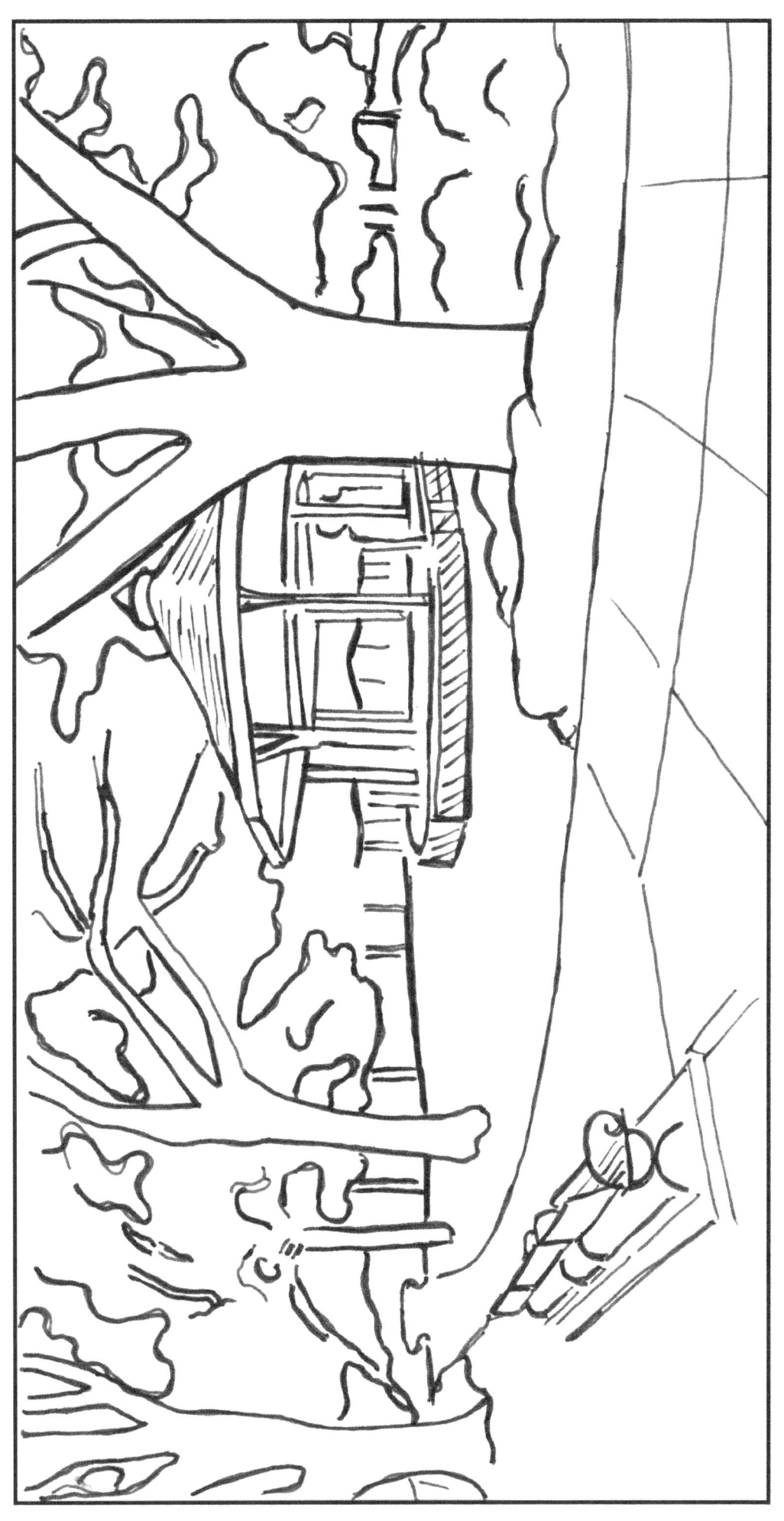

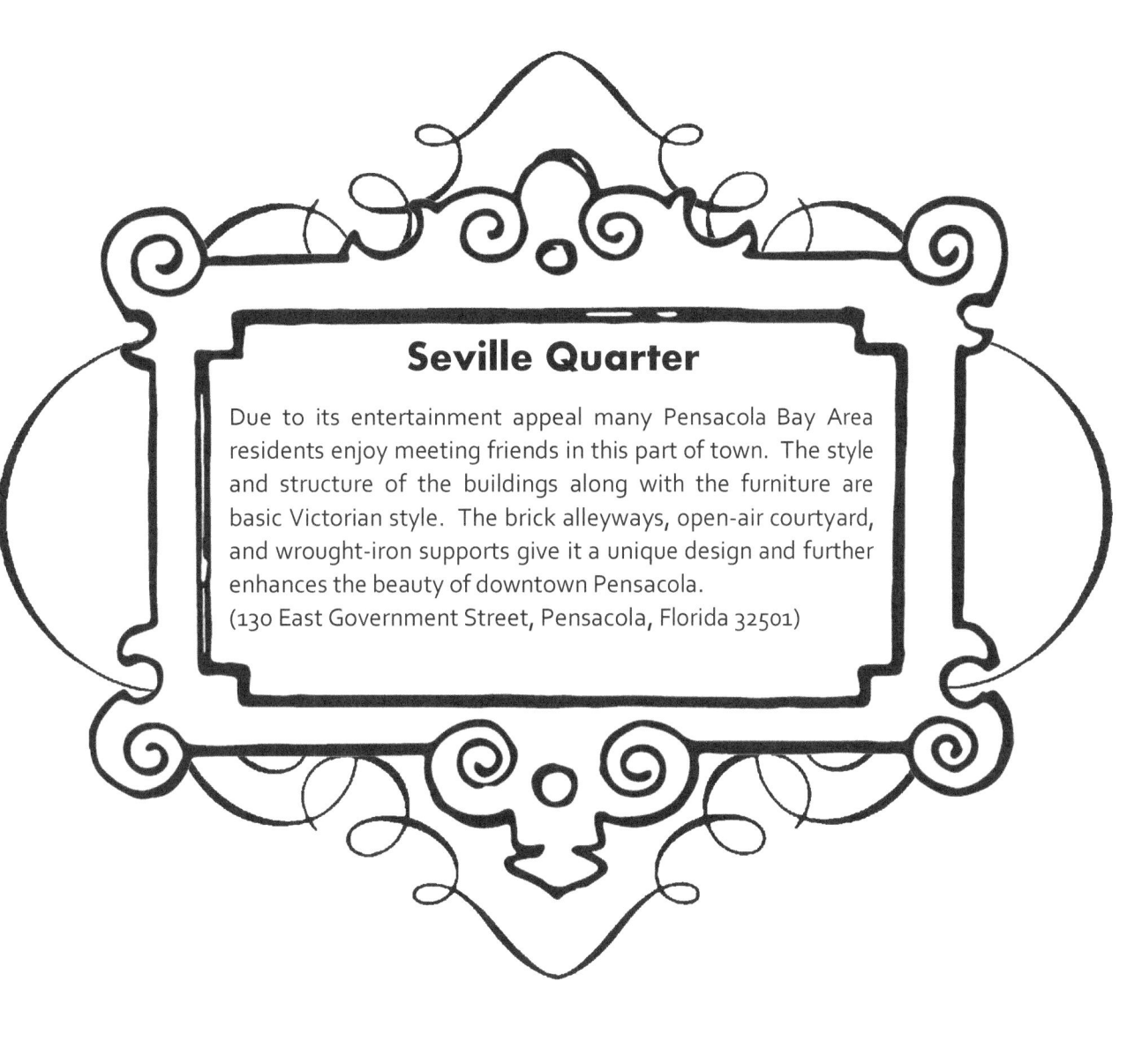

Seville Quarter

Due to its entertainment appeal many Pensacola Bay Area residents enjoy meeting friends in this part of town. The style and structure of the buildings along with the furniture are basic Victorian style. The brick alleyways, open-air courtyard, and wrought-iron supports give it a unique design and further enhances the beauty of downtown Pensacola.

(130 East Government Street, Pensacola, Florida 32501)

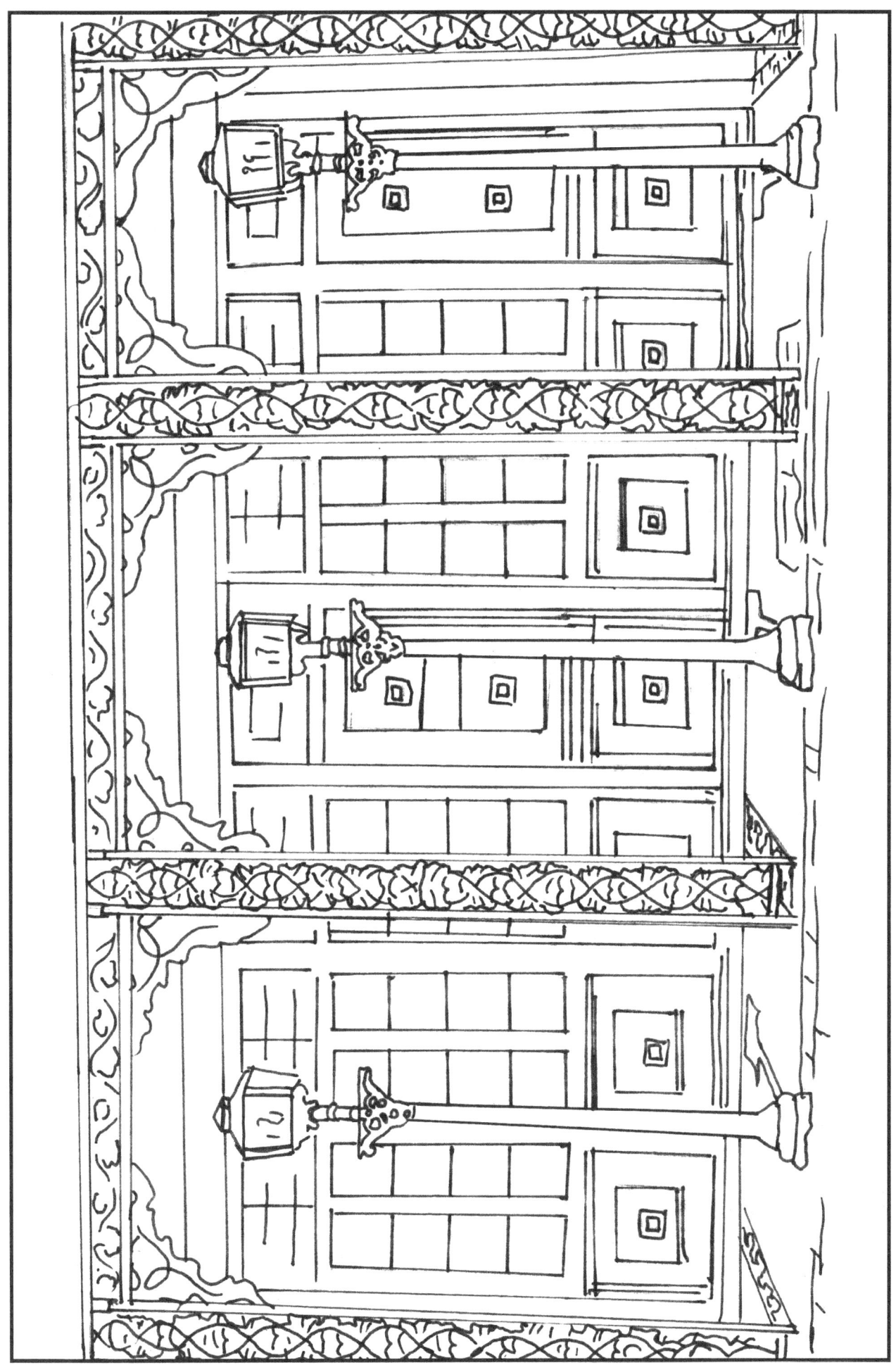

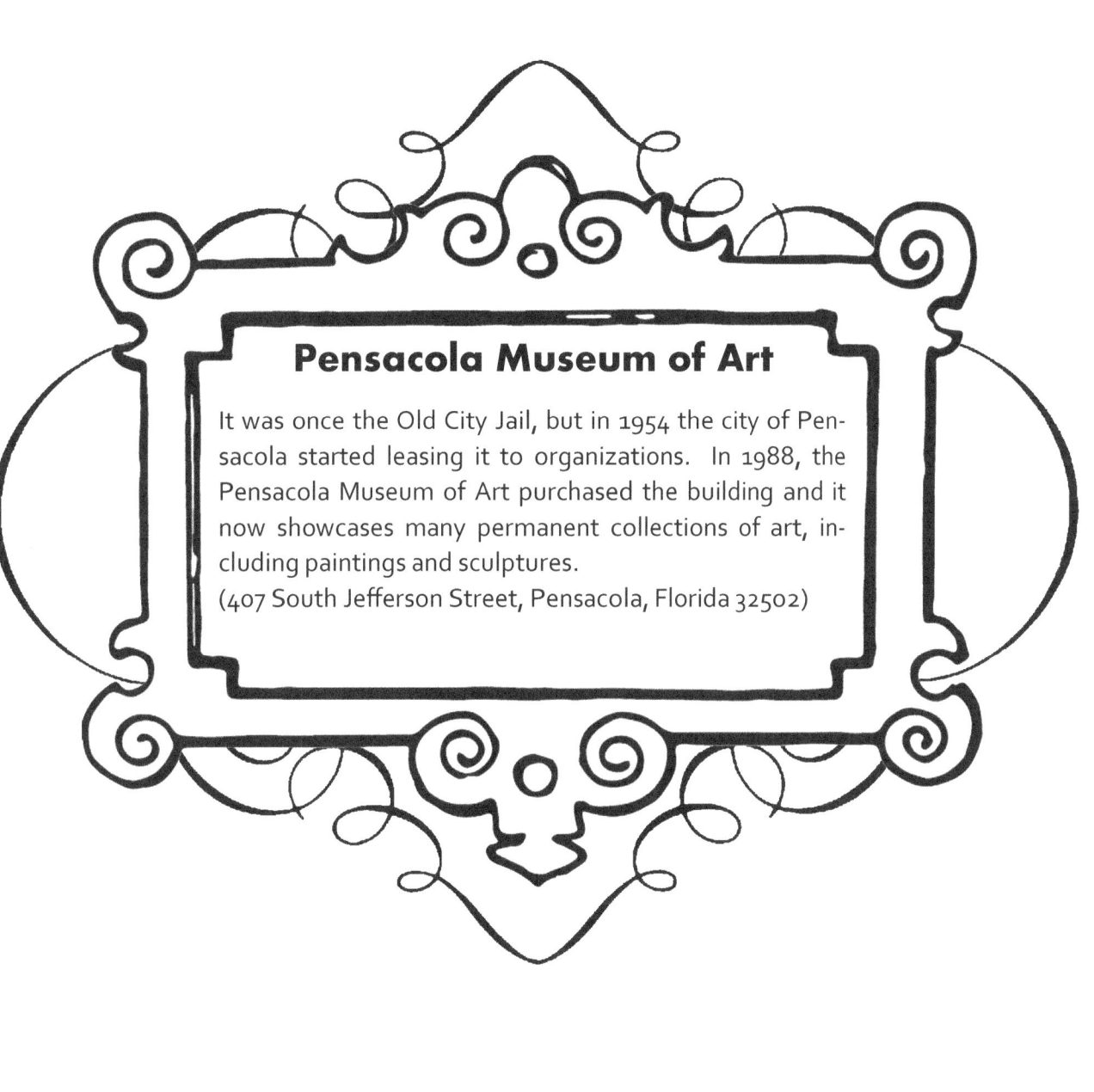

Pensacola Museum of Art

It was once the Old City Jail, but in 1954 the city of Pensacola started leasing it to organizations. In 1988, the Pensacola Museum of Art purchased the building and it now showcases many permanent collections of art, including paintings and sculptures.

(407 South Jefferson Street, Pensacola, Florida 32502)

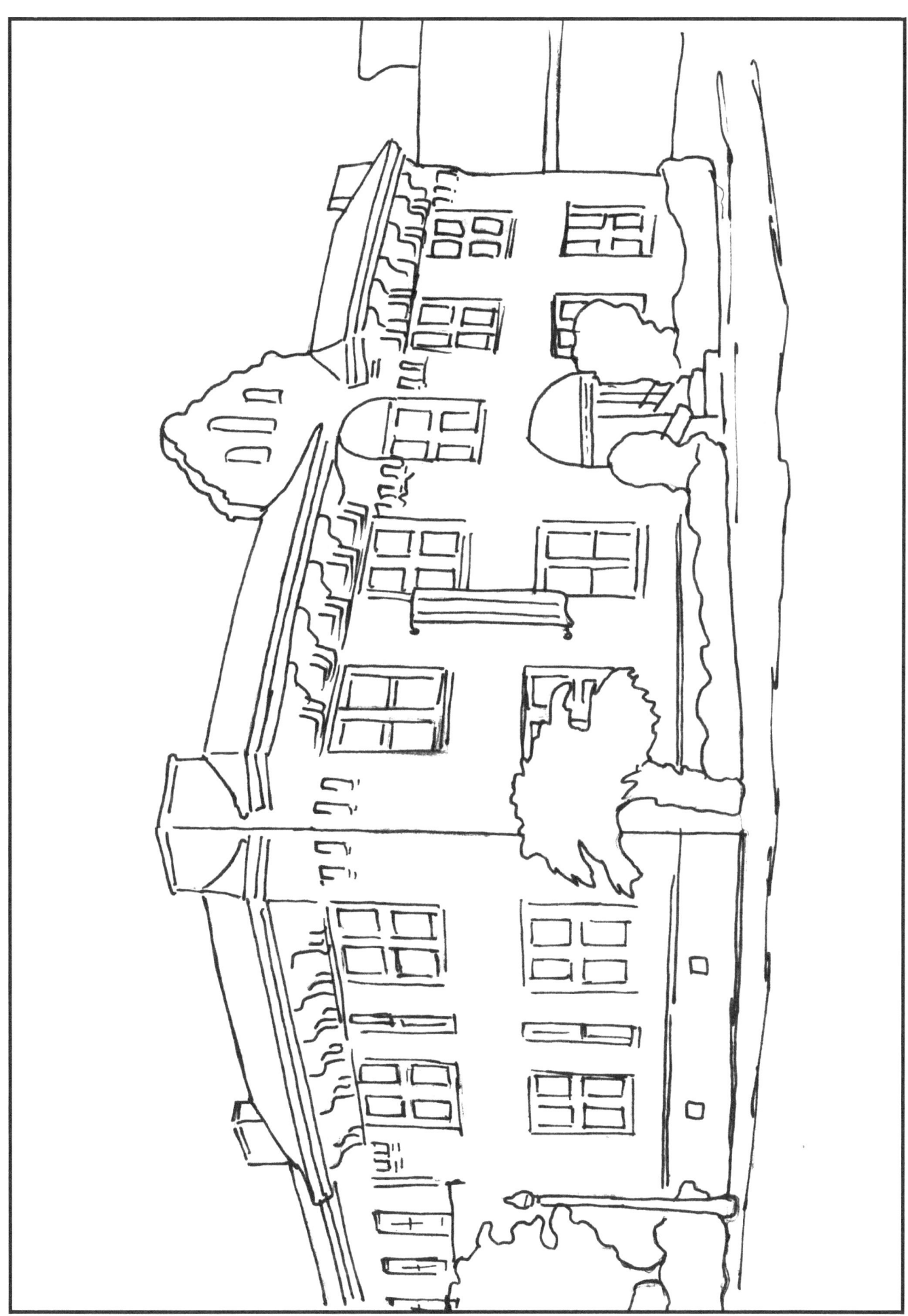

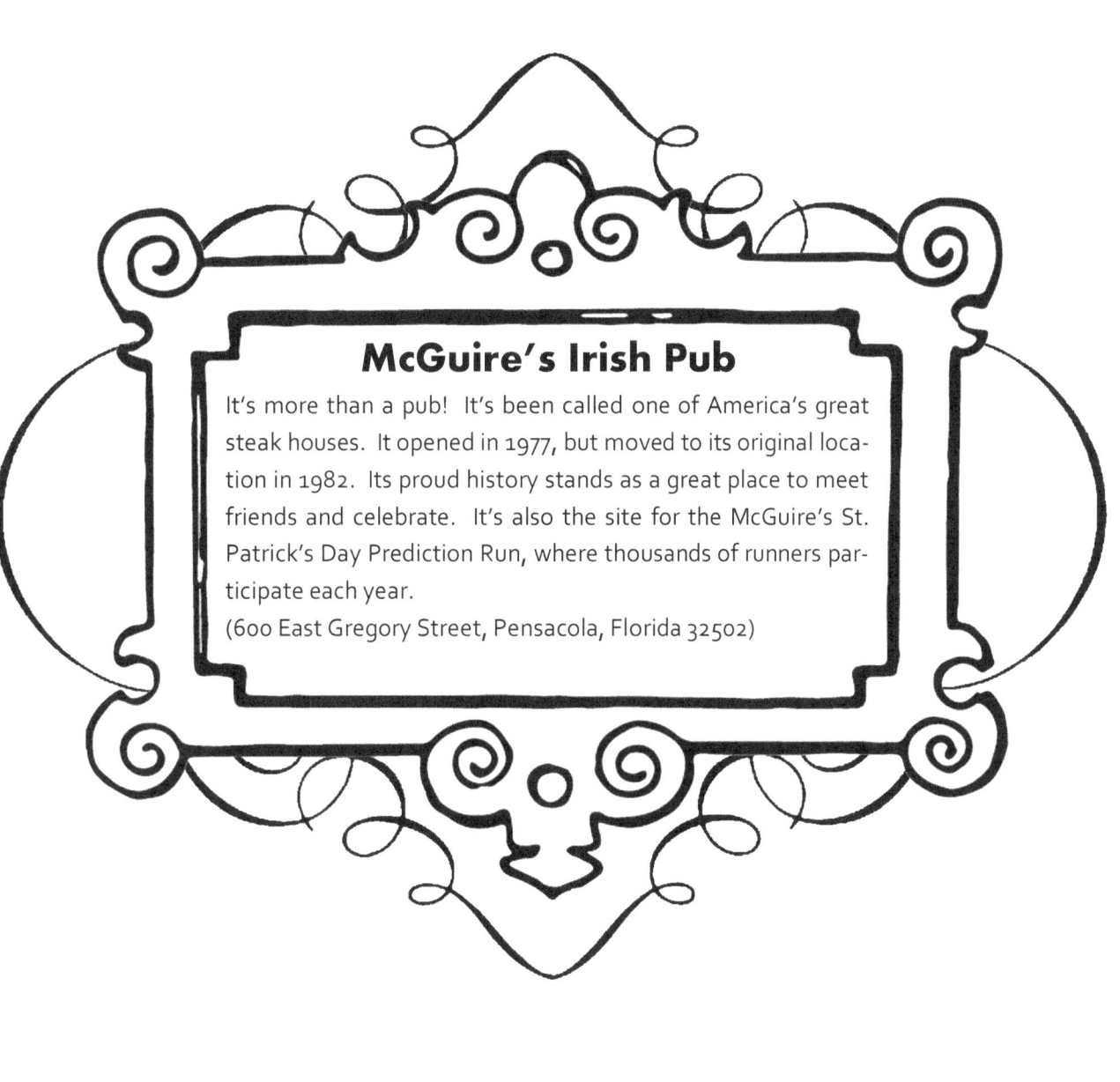

McGuire's Irish Pub

It's more than a pub! It's been called one of America's great steak houses. It opened in 1977, but moved to its original location in 1982. Its proud history stands as a great place to meet friends and celebrate. It's also the site for the McGuire's St. Patrick's Day Prediction Run, where thousands of runners participate each year.

(600 East Gregory Street, Pensacola, Florida 32502)

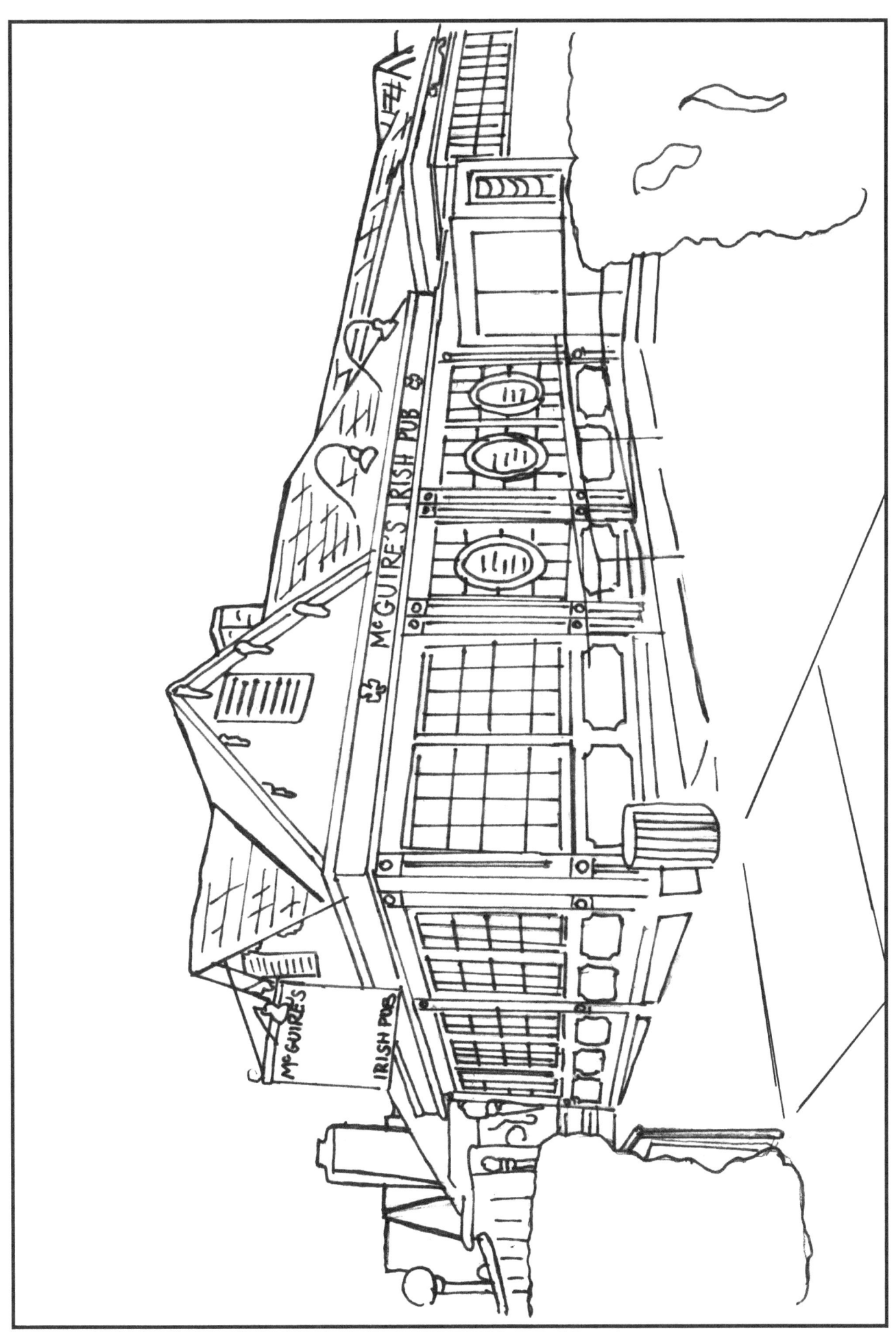

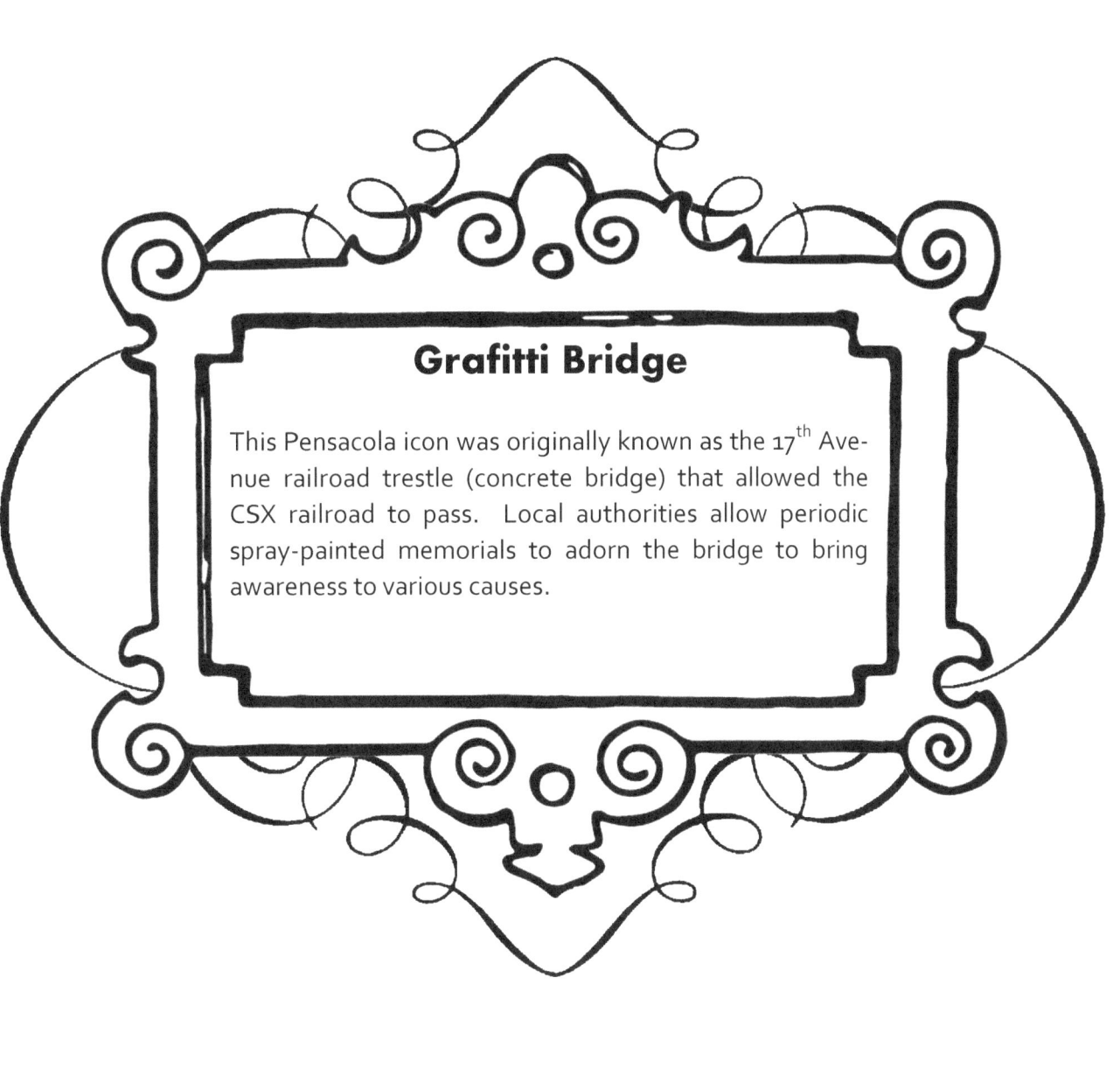

Grafitti Bridge

This Pensacola icon was originally known as the 17th Avenue railroad trestle (concrete bridge) that allowed the CSX railroad to pass. Local authorities allow periodic spray-painted memorials to adorn the bridge to bring awareness to various causes.

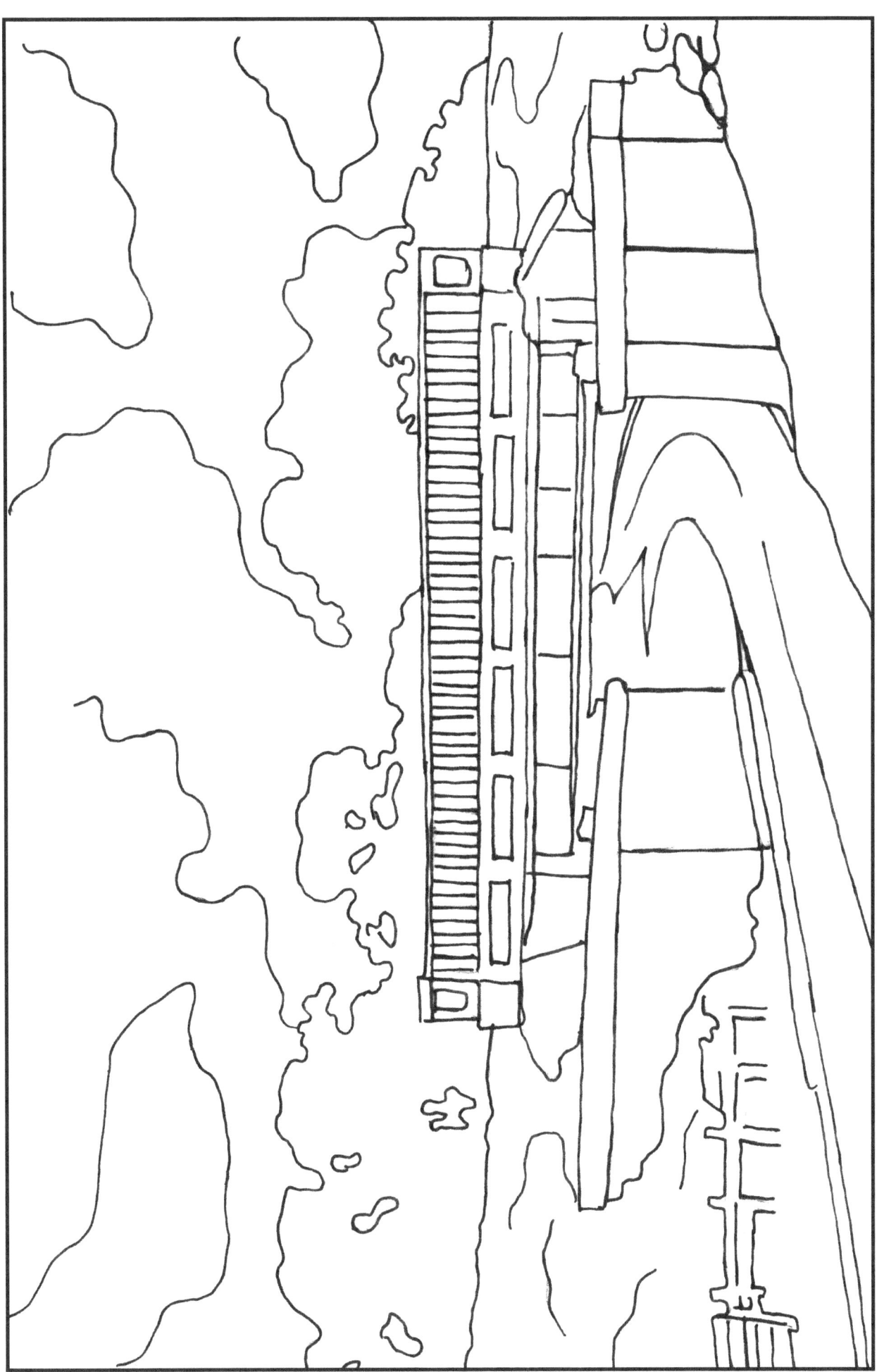

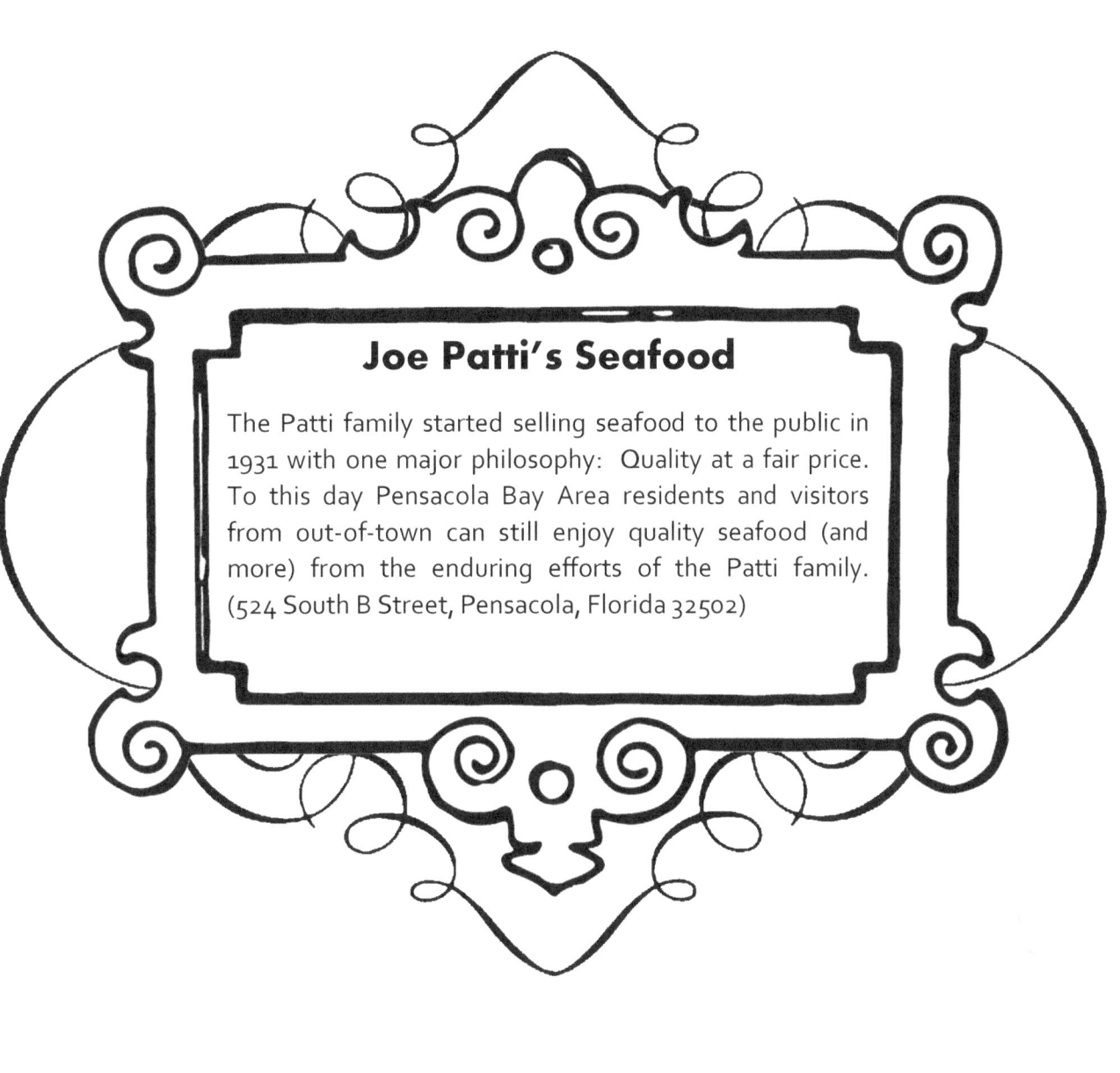

Joe Patti's Seafood

The Patti family started selling seafood to the public in 1931 with one major philosophy: Quality at a fair price. To this day Pensacola Bay Area residents and visitors from out-of-town can still enjoy quality seafood (and more) from the enduring efforts of the Patti family. (524 South B Street, Pensacola, Florida 32502)

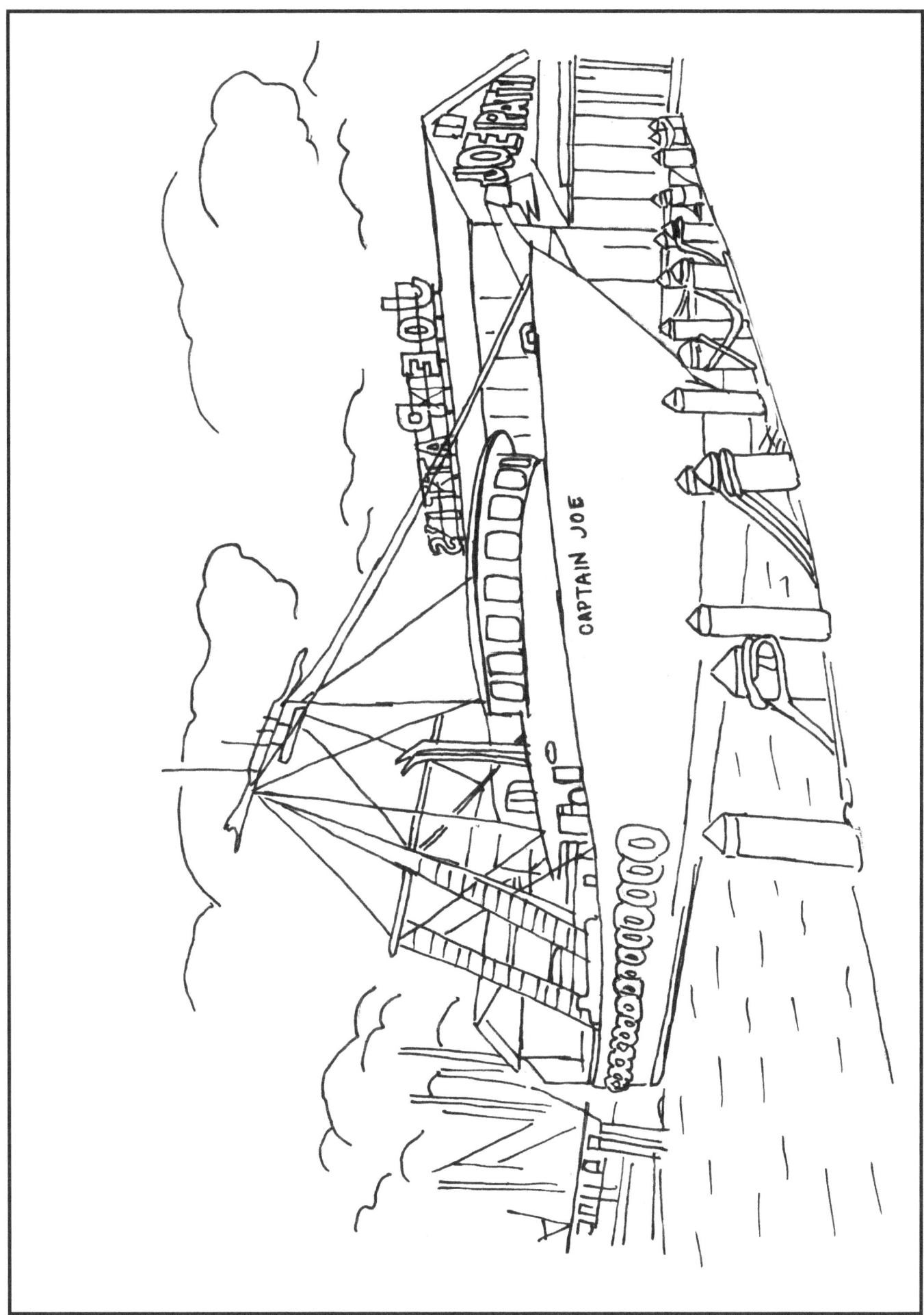

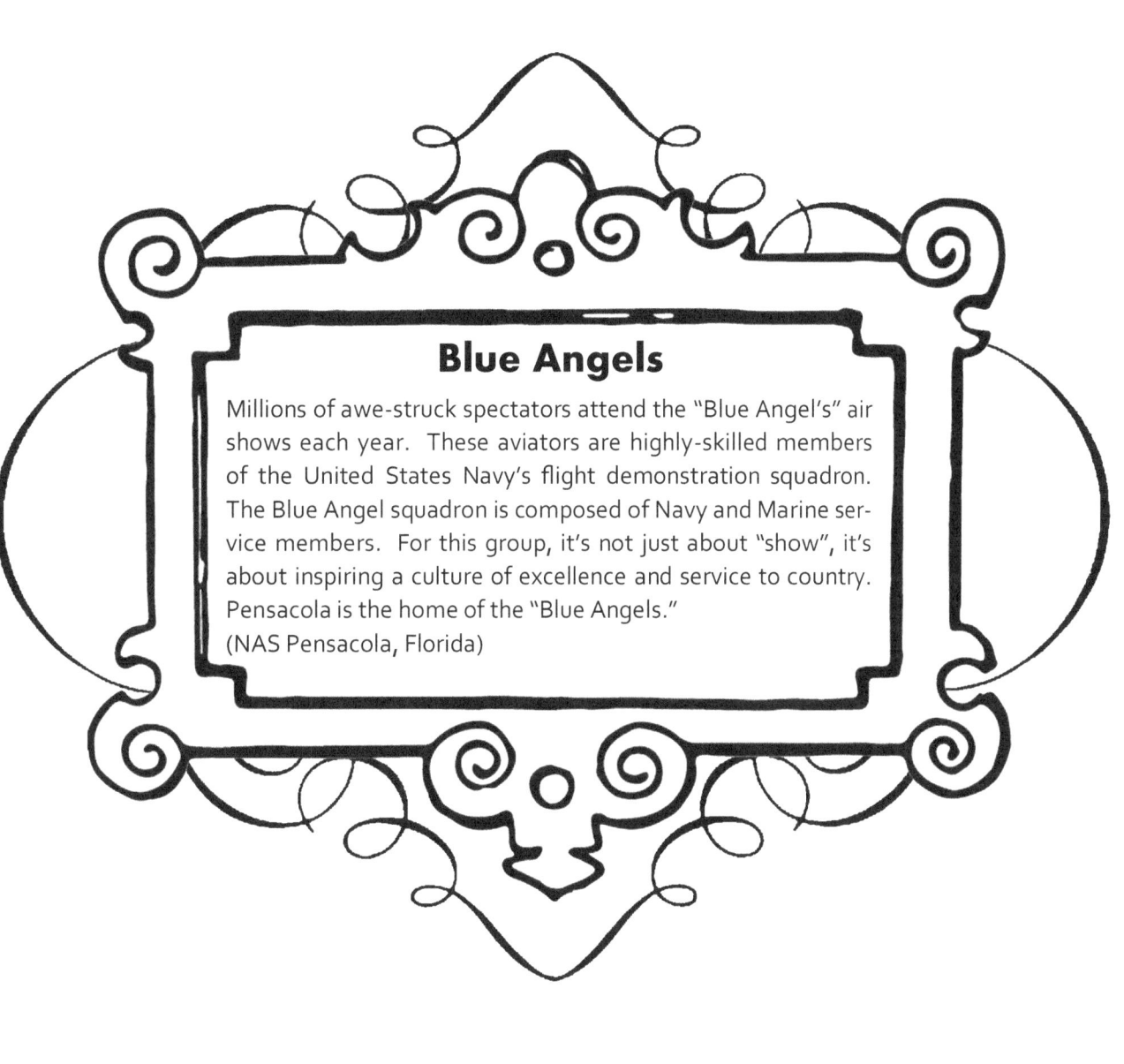

Blue Angels

Millions of awe-struck spectators attend the "Blue Angel's" air shows each year. These aviators are highly-skilled members of the United States Navy's flight demonstration squadron. The Blue Angel squadron is composed of Navy and Marine service members. For this group, it's not just about "show", it's about inspiring a culture of excellence and service to country. Pensacola is the home of the "Blue Angels."

(NAS Pensacola, Florida)

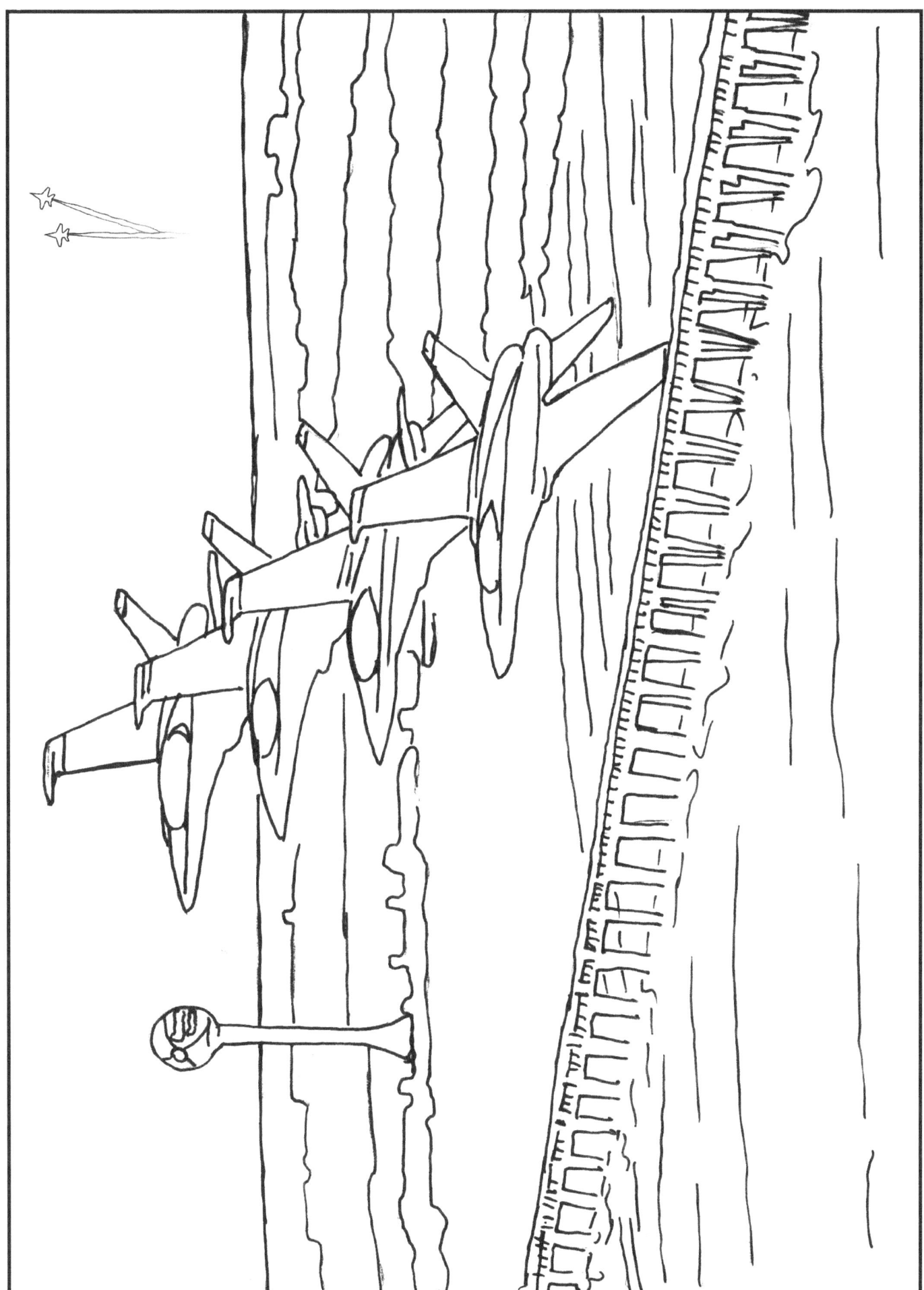

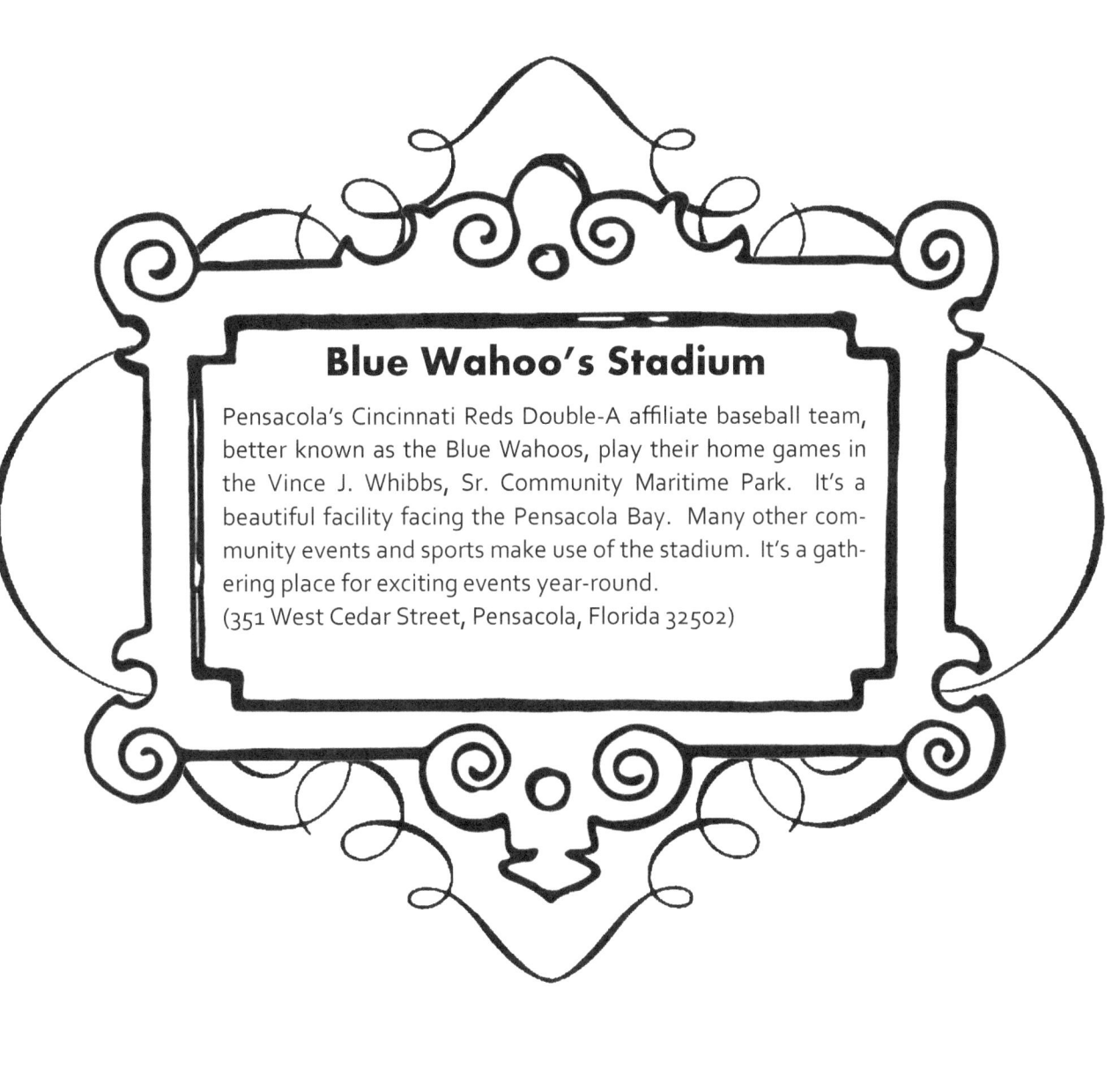

Blue Wahoo's Stadium

Pensacola's Cincinnati Reds Double-A affiliate baseball team, better known as the Blue Wahoos, play their home games in the Vince J. Whibbs, Sr. Community Maritime Park. It's a beautiful facility facing the Pensacola Bay. Many other community events and sports make use of the stadium. It's a gathering place for exciting events year-round.

(351 West Cedar Street, Pensacola, Florida 32502)

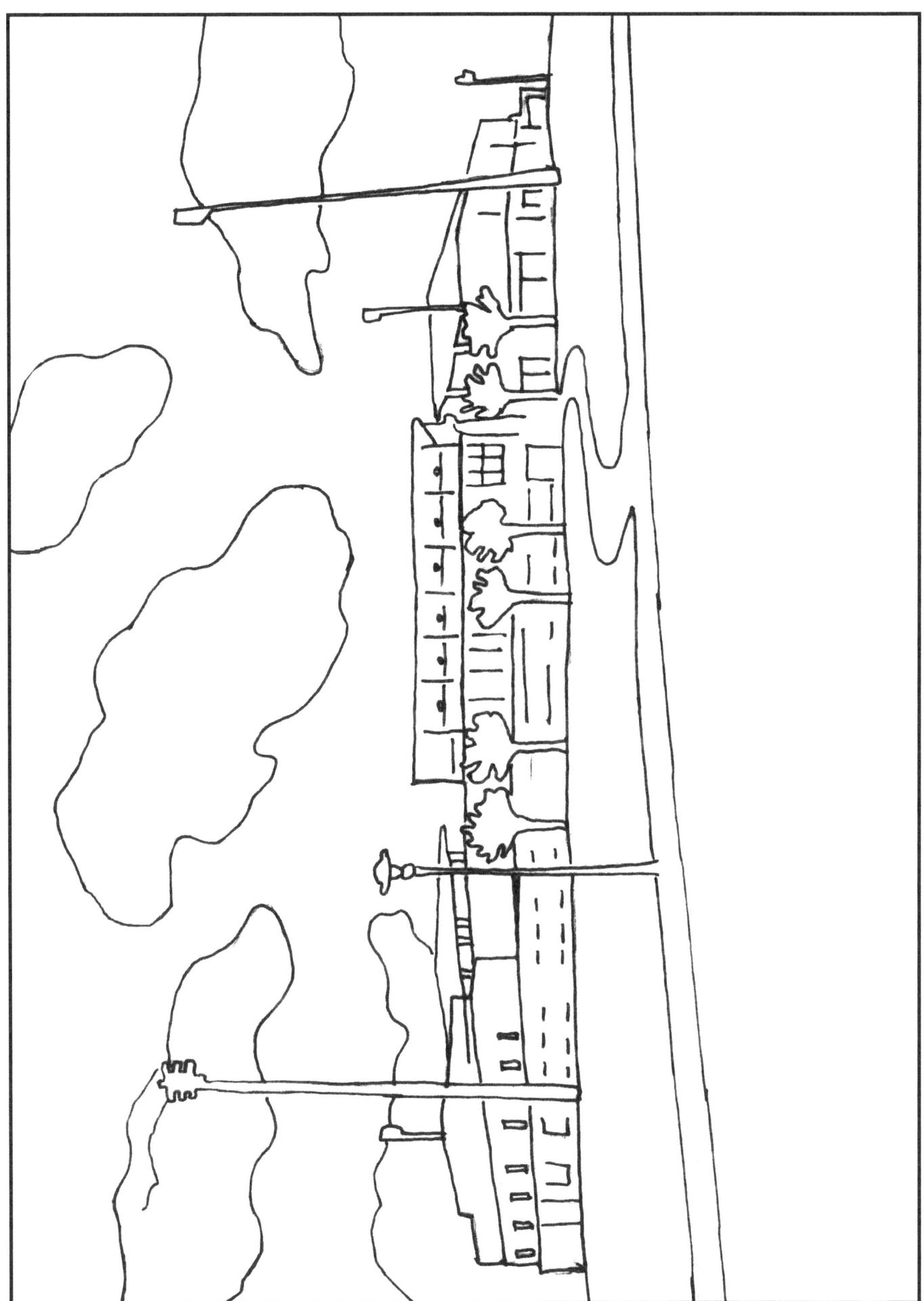

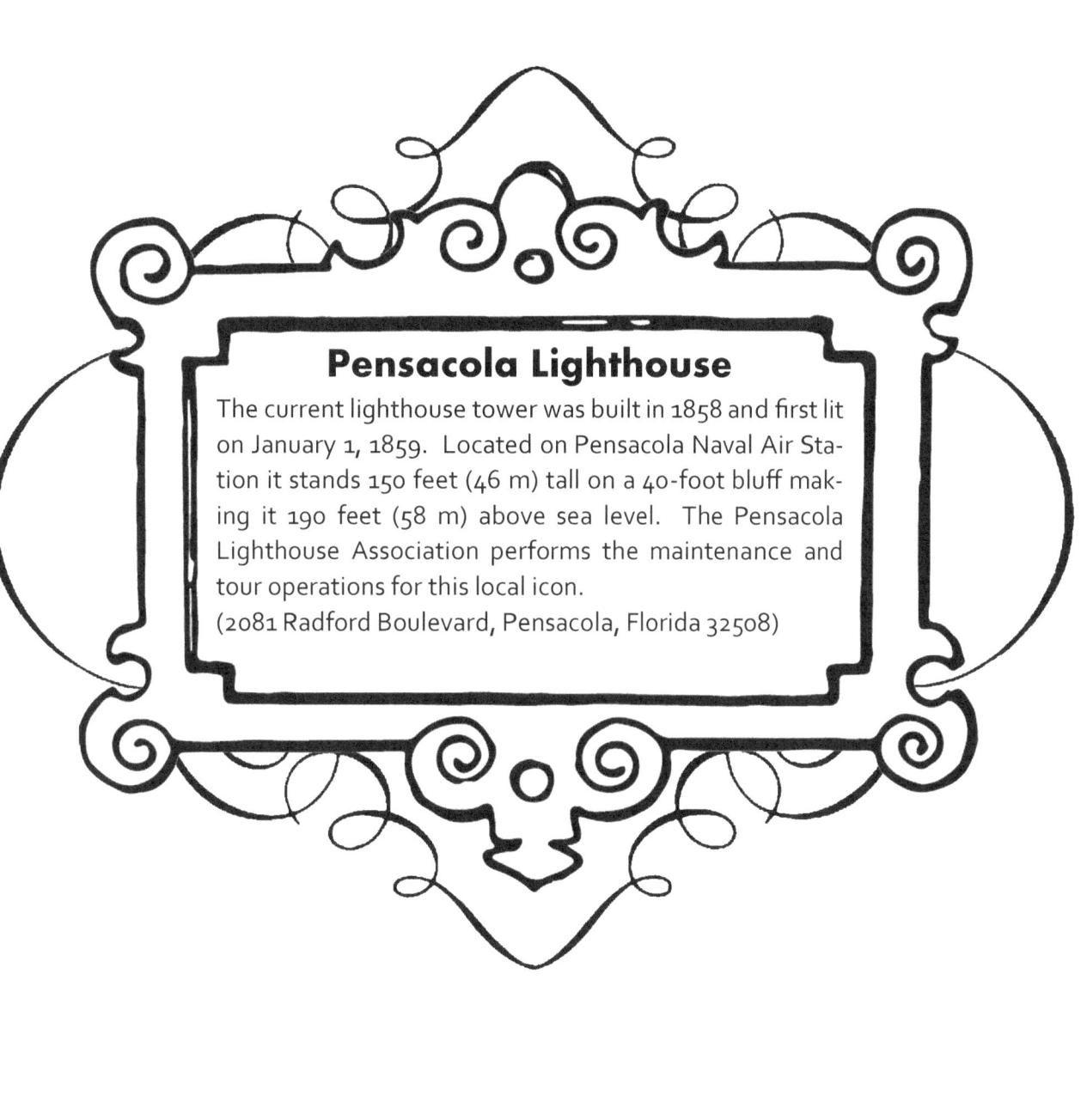

Pensacola Lighthouse

The current lighthouse tower was built in 1858 and first lit on January 1, 1859. Located on Pensacola Naval Air Station it stands 150 feet (46 m) tall on a 40-foot bluff making it 190 feet (58 m) above sea level. The Pensacola Lighthouse Association performs the maintenance and tour operations for this local icon.

(2081 Radford Boulevard, Pensacola, Florida 32508)

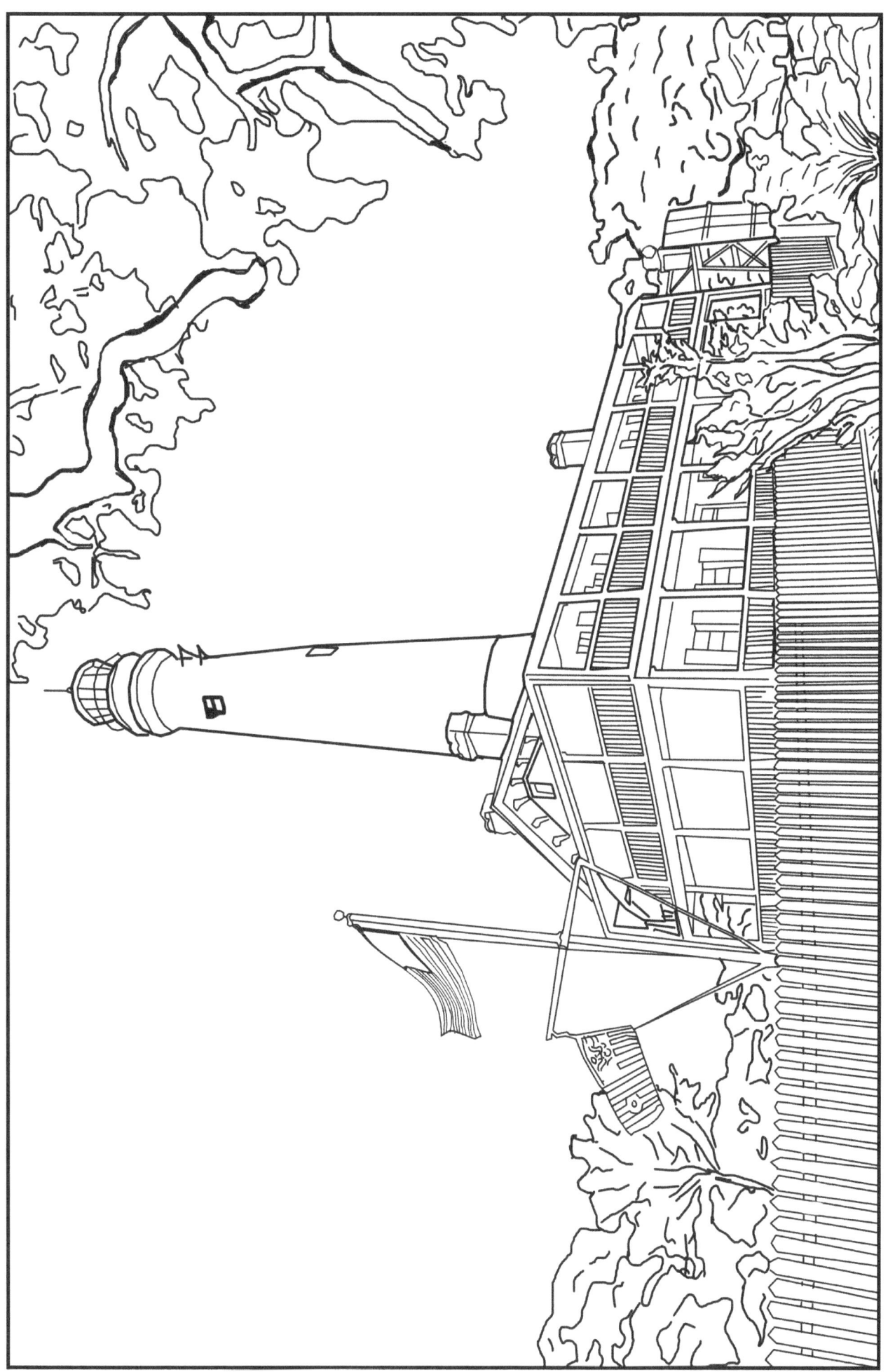

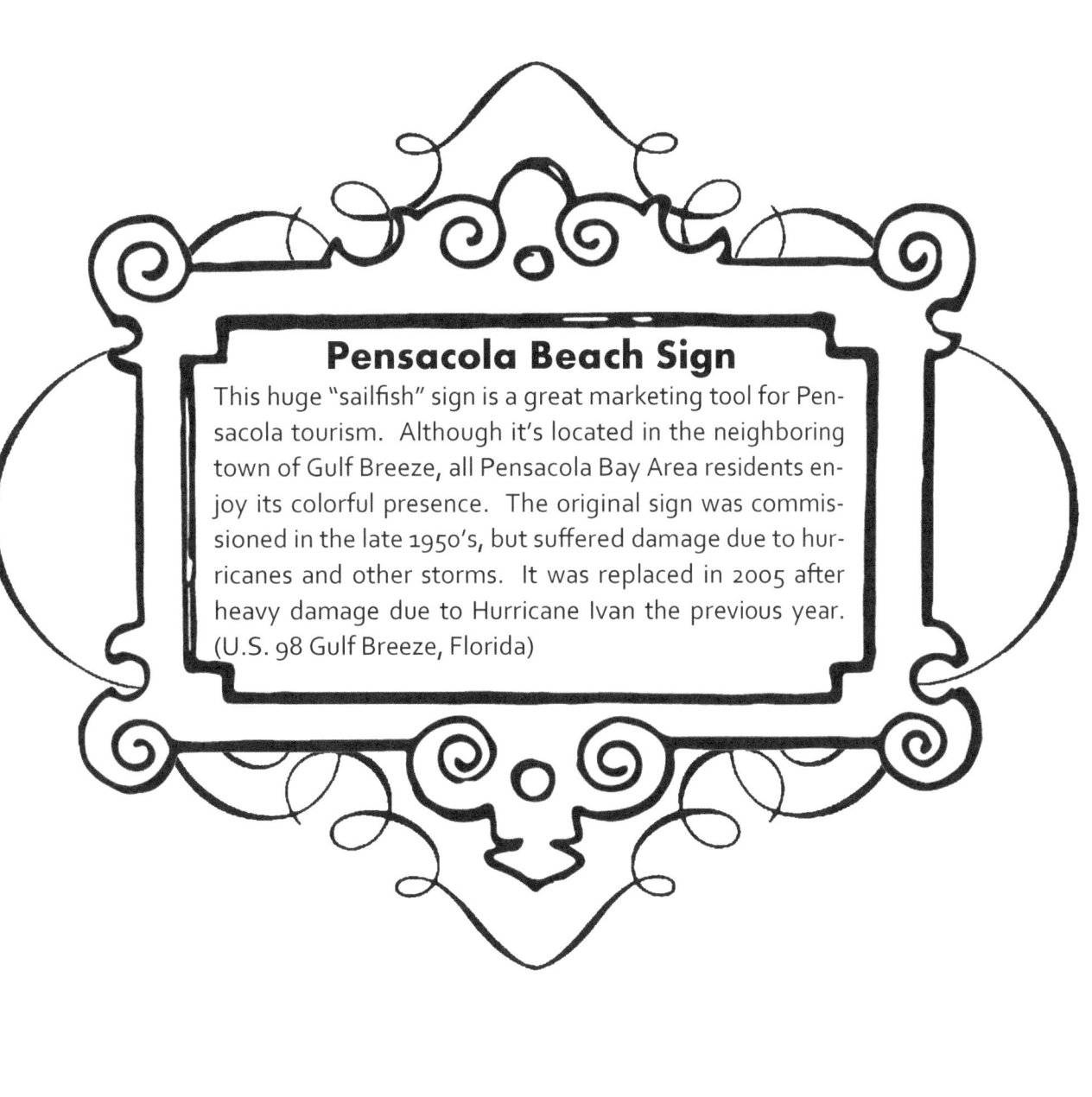

Pensacola Beach Sign

This huge "sailfish" sign is a great marketing tool for Pensacola tourism. Although it's located in the neighboring town of Gulf Breeze, all Pensacola Bay Area residents enjoy its colorful presence. The original sign was commissioned in the late 1950's, but suffered damage due to hurricanes and other storms. It was replaced in 2005 after heavy damage due to Hurricane Ivan the previous year. (U.S. 98 Gulf Breeze, Florida)

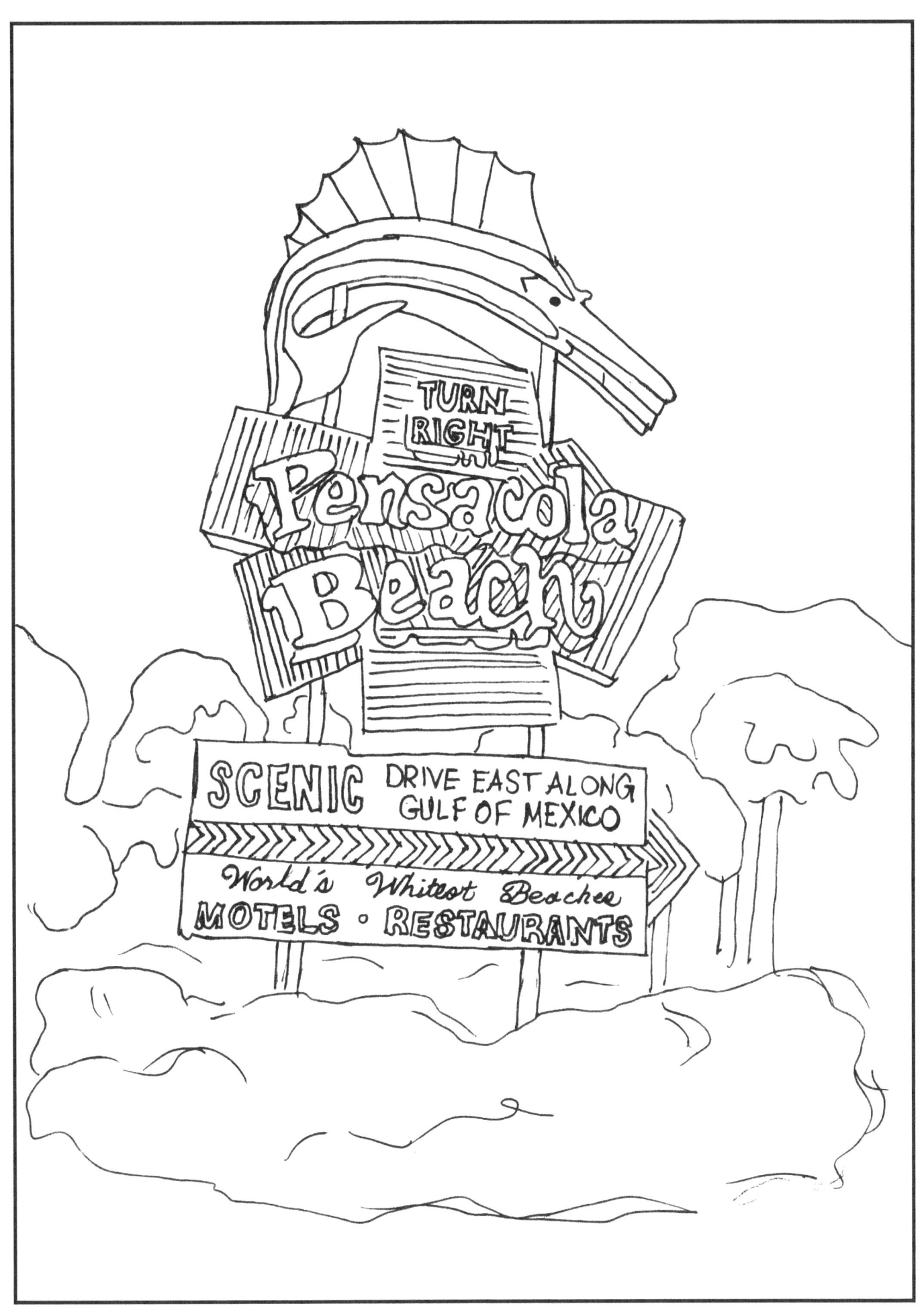

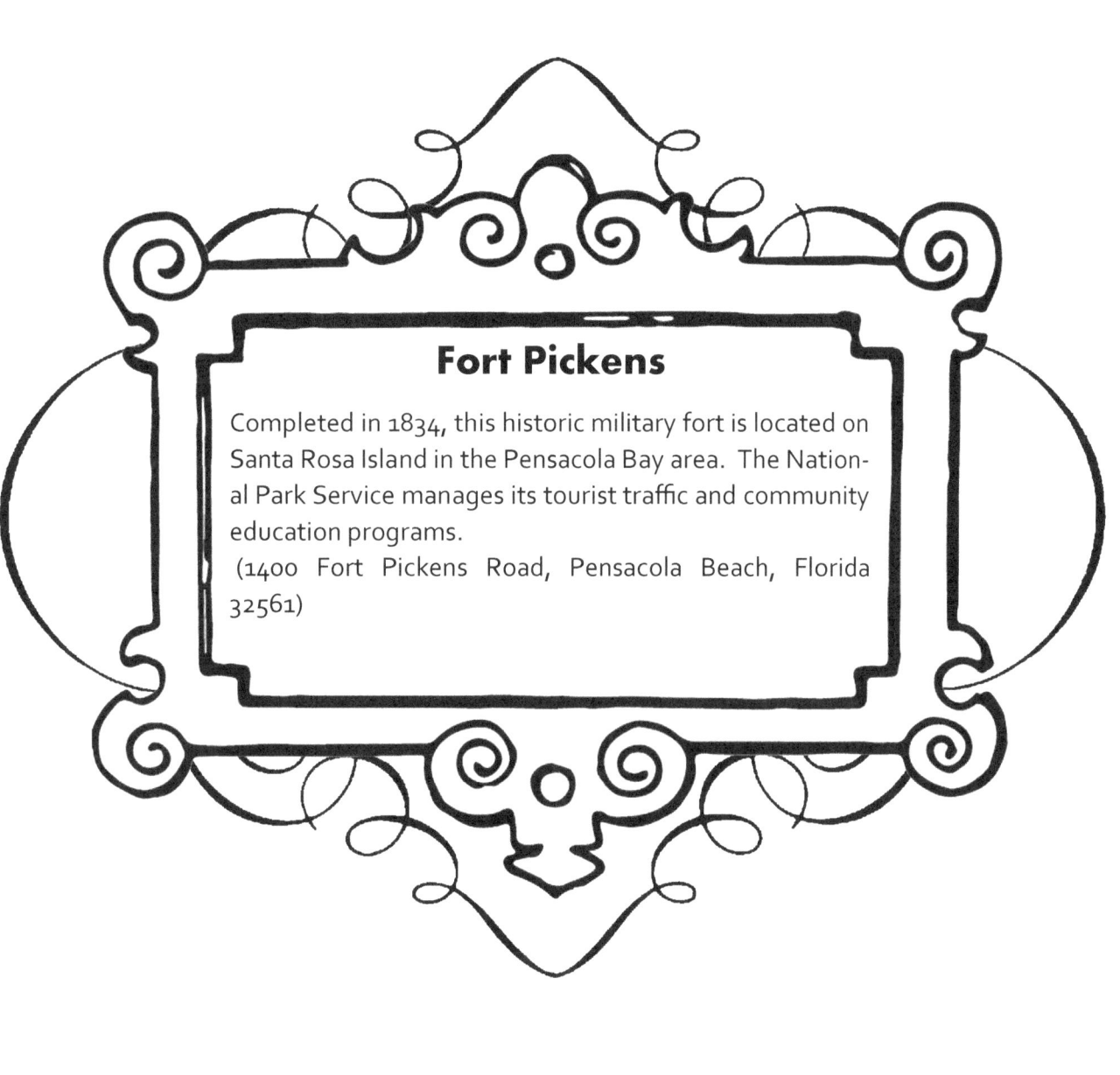

Fort Pickens

Completed in 1834, this historic military fort is located on Santa Rosa Island in the Pensacola Bay area. The National Park Service manages its tourist traffic and community education programs.

(1400 Fort Pickens Road, Pensacola Beach, Florida 32561)

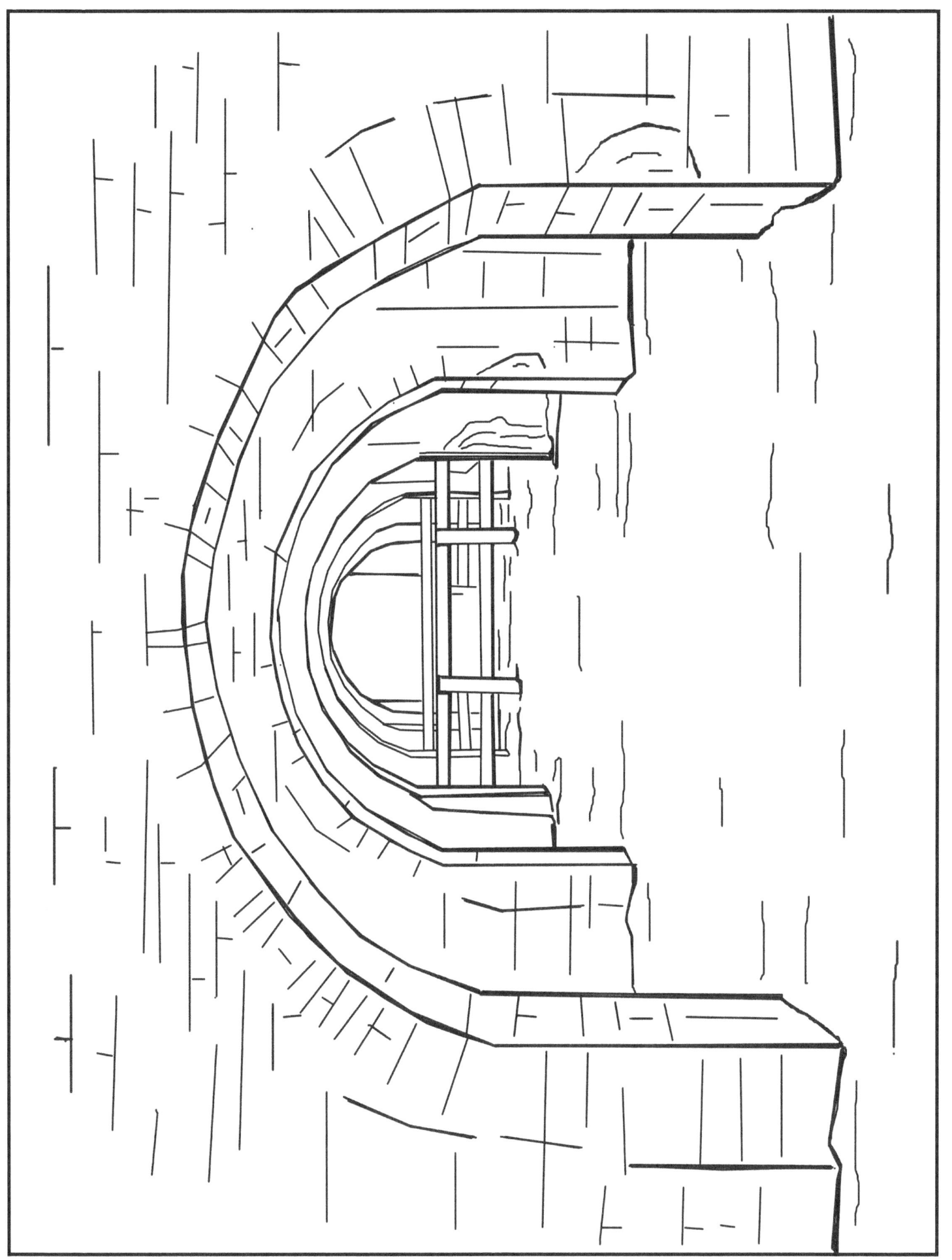

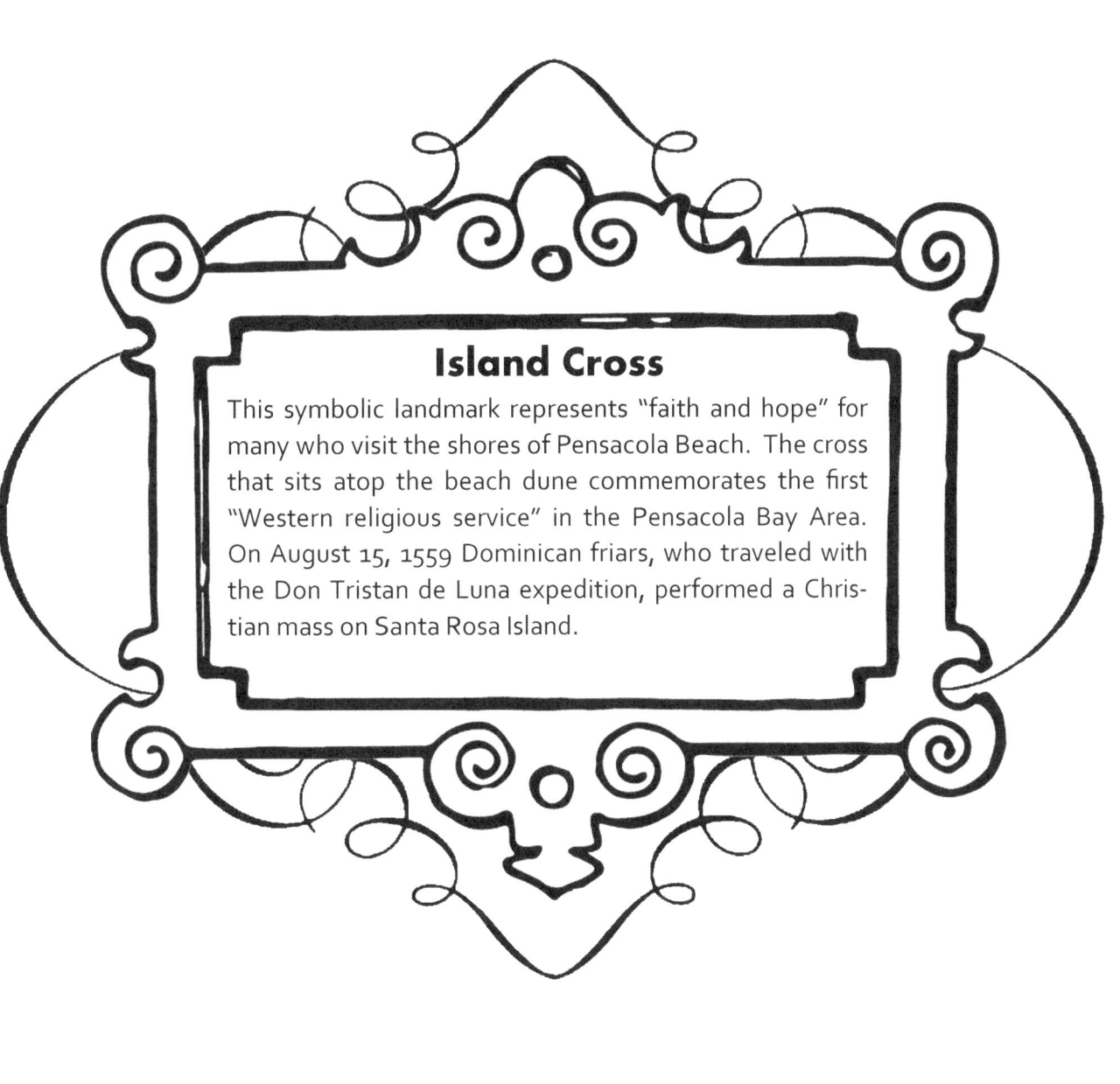

Island Cross

This symbolic landmark represents "faith and hope" for many who visit the shores of Pensacola Beach. The cross that sits atop the beach dune commemorates the first "Western religious service" in the Pensacola Bay Area. On August 15, 1559 Dominican friars, who traveled with the Don Tristan de Luna expedition, performed a Christian mass on Santa Rosa Island.

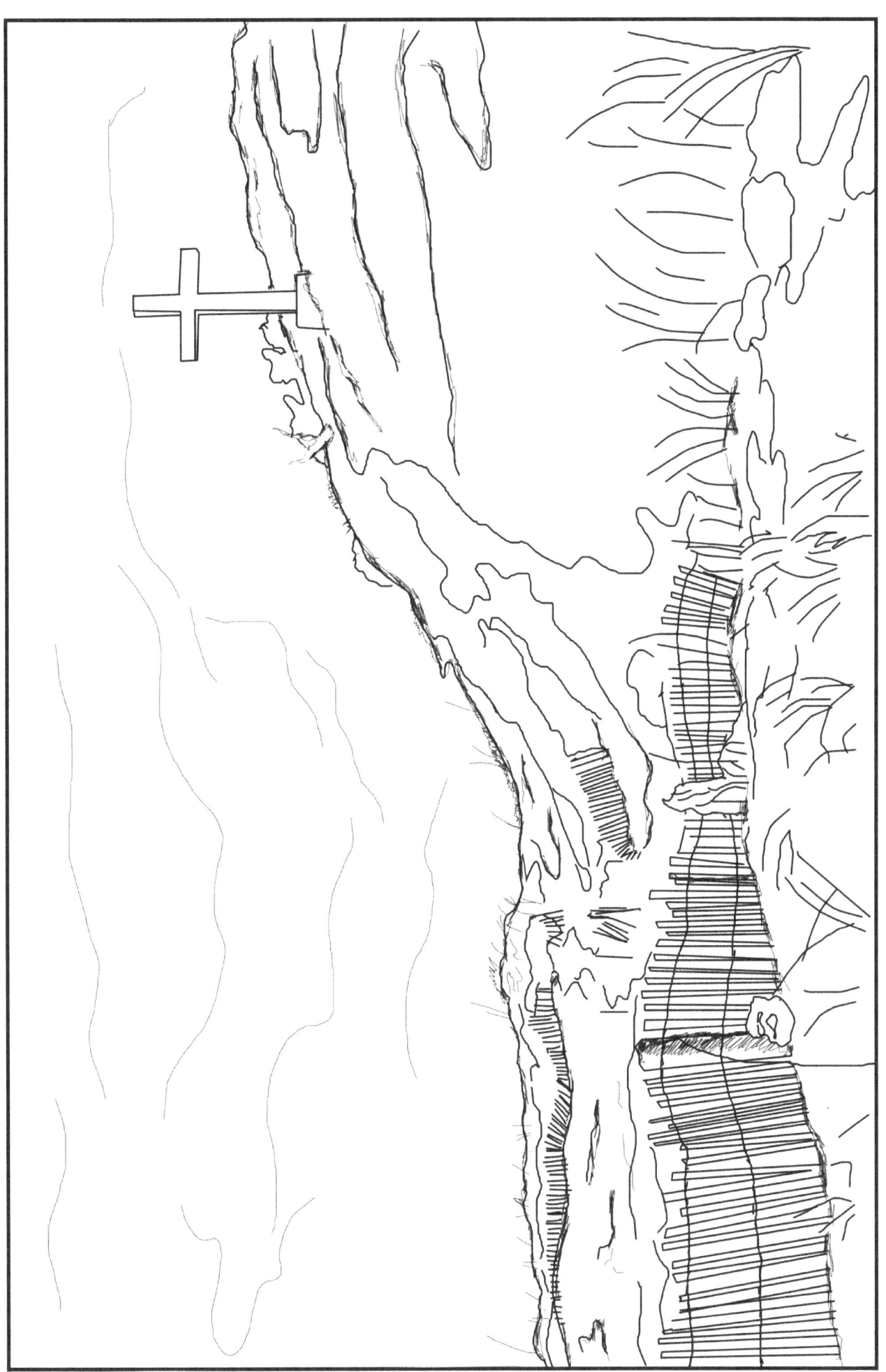

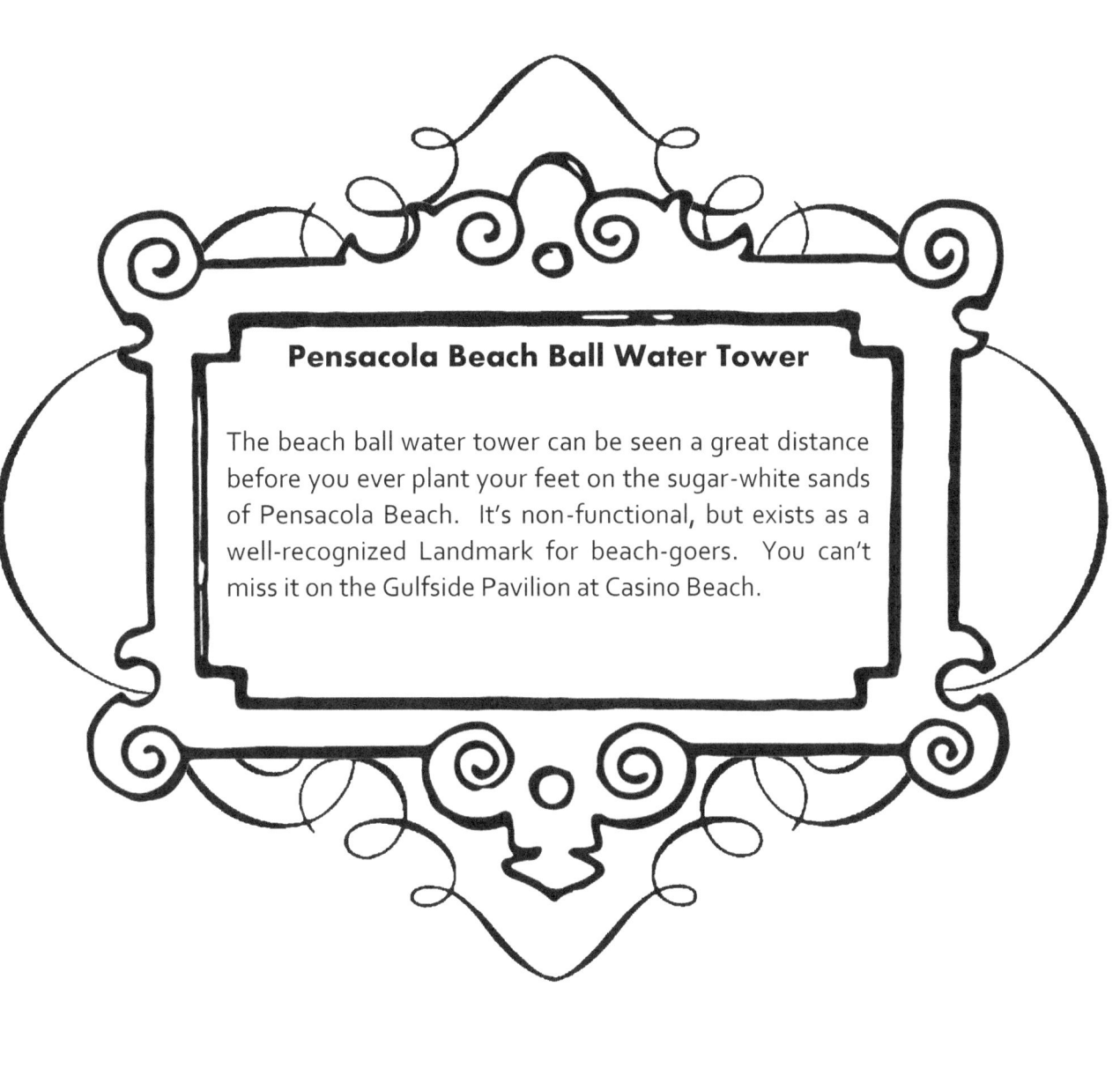

Pensacola Beach Ball Water Tower

The beach ball water tower can be seen a great distance before you ever plant your feet on the sugar-white sands of Pensacola Beach. It's non-functional, but exists as a well-recognized Landmark for beach-goers. You can't miss it on the Gulfside Pavilion at Casino Beach.

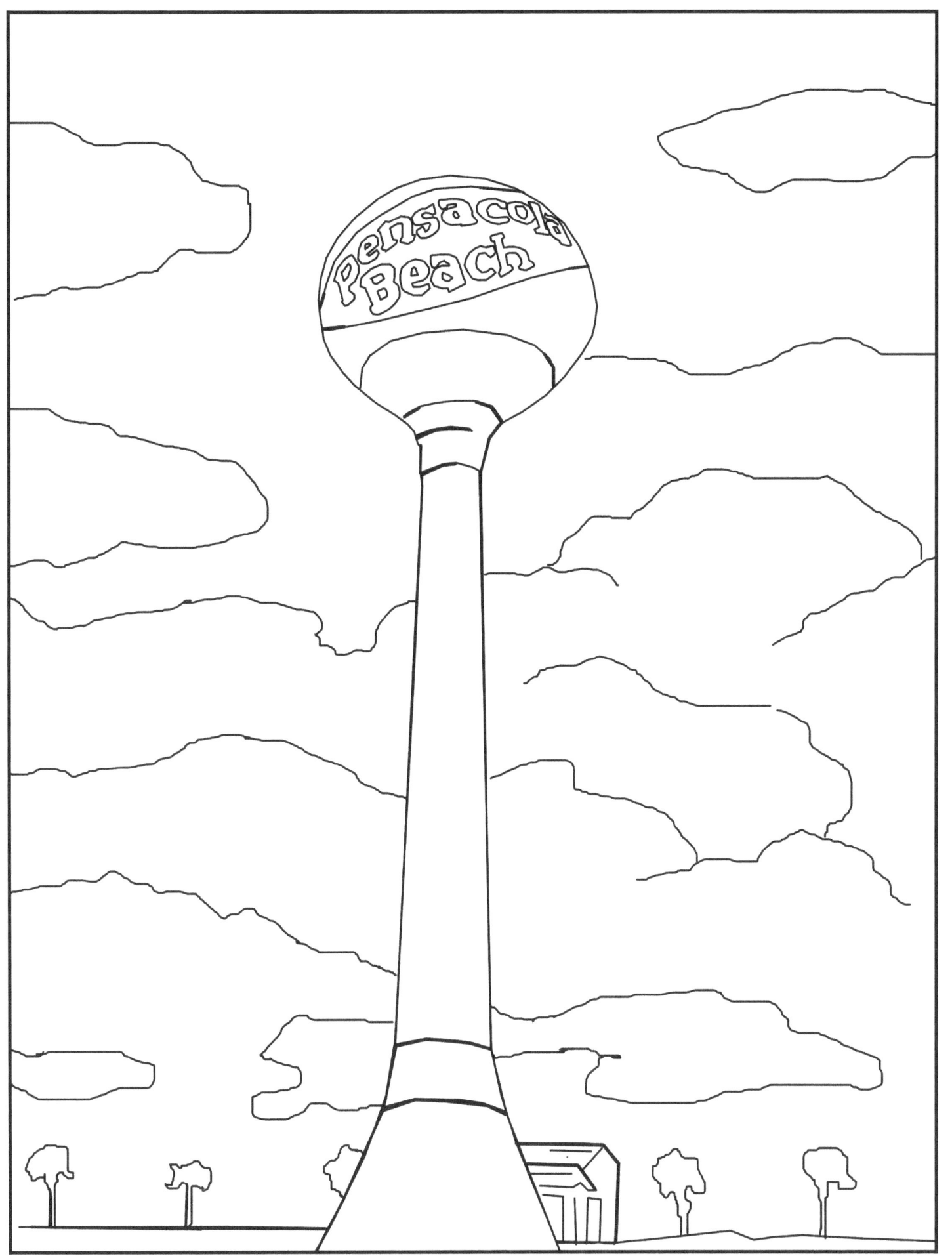

www.ingramcontent.com/pod-product-compliance
Lightning Source LLC
Chambersburg PA
CBHW081120180526
45170CB00008B/2942